Privacy in the UK

Series Editor: Cara Acred

Volume 245

Independence Educational Publishers

First published by Independence Educational Publishers

The Studio, High Green

Great Shelford

Cambridge CB22 5EG

England

© Independence 2013

Copyright

This book is sold subject to the condition that it shall not,

by way of trade or otherwise, be lent, resold, hired out or otherwise

circulated in any form of binding or cover other than that in which it

is published without the publisher's prior consent.

Photocopy licence

The material in this book is protected by copyright. However, the

purchaser is free to make multiple copies of particular articles for instructional

purposes for immediate use within the purchasing institution.

Making copies of the entire book is not permitted.

British Library Cataloguing in Publication Data

Privacy in the UK. -- (Issues ; 245)

1. Privacy, Right of--Great Britain. 2. Data protection--

Law and legislation--Great Britain. 3. Electronic

surveillance--Great Britain.

I. Series II. Acred, Cara editor of compilation.

323.4'48-dc23

ISBN-13: 978 1 86168 647 3

Printed in Great Britain

MWL Print Group Ltd

Contents

Introduction

Privacy in the UK is Volume 245 in the **ISSUES** series. The aim of the series is to offer current, diverse information about important issues in our world, from a UK perspective.

ABOUT PRIVACY IN THE UK

How often do you think about the concept of privacy? In all likelihood, not very often. However, in today's digitally driven society, it is important that we are aware of how our actions are monitored and our personal histories stored. What do you know about data protection and privacy laws? How would you feel if all your text messages, emails and Internet searches were saved and available to Government bodies at the click of a button? Privacy in the UK explores these issues, considering both positive and negative viewpoints.

OUR SOURCES

Titles in the **ISSUES** series are designed to function as educational resource books, providing a balanced overview of a specific subject.

The information in our books is comprised of facts, articles and opinions from many different sources, including:

- Newspaper reports and opinion pieces
- Website factsheets
- Magazine and journal articles
- Statistics and surveys
- Government reports
- Literature from special interest groups

A NOTE ON CRITICAL EVALUATION

Because the information reprinted here is from a number of different sources, readers should bear in mind the origin of the text and whether the source is likely to have a particular bias when presenting information (or when conducting their research). It is hoped that, as you read about the many aspects of the issues explored in this book, you will critically evaluate the information presented.

It is important that you decide whether you are being presented with facts or opinions. Does the writer give a biased or unbiased report? If an opinion is being expressed, do you agree with the writer? Is there potential bias to the 'facts' or statistics behind an article?

ASSIGNMENTS

In the back of this book, you will find a selection of assignments designed to help you engage with the articles you have been reading and to explore your own opinions. Some tasks will take longer than others and there is a mixture of design, writing and research-based activities that you can complete alone or in a group.

FURTHER RESEARCH

At the end of each article we have listed its source and a website that you can visit if you would like to conduct your own research. Please remember to critically evaluate any sources that you consult and consider whether the information you are viewing is accurate and unbiased.

Right to a private and family life

Everyone has the right to respect for his or her private and family life, home and correspondence. This right is subject to proportionate and lawful restrictions.

Article 8 of the UK's Human Rights Act is a broad-ranging right that is often closely connected with other rights such as freedom of religion, freedom of expression, freedom of association and the right to respect for property.

The obligation on the State under Article 8 is to refrain from interfering with the right itself and also to take some positive measures, for example, to criminalise extreme breaches of the right to a private life by private individuals.

Private life

The concept of a right to a private life encompasses the importance of personal dignity and autonomy and the interaction a person has with others, both in private or in public.

Respect for one's private life includes:

⇨ respect for individual sexuality (so, for example, investigations into the sexuality of members of the armed forces engages the right to respect for a private life);

⇨ the right to personal autonomy and physical and psychological integrity, i.e. the right not to be physically interfered with;

⇨ respect for private and confidential information, particularly the storing and sharing of such information;

⇨ the right not to be subject to unlawful state surveillance;

⇨ respect for privacy when one has a reasonable expectation of privacy; and

⇨ the right to control the dissemination of information about one's private life, including photographs taken covertly.

Family life

Article 8 also provides the right to respect for one's established family life. This includes close family ties, although there is no pre-determined model of a family or family life. It includes any stable relationship, be it married, engaged, or de facto; between parents and children; siblings; grandparents and grandchildren, etc. This right is often engaged, for example, when measures are taken by the State to separate family members (by removing children into care, or deporting one member of a family group).

Respect for the home

Right to respect for the home includes a right not to have one's home life interfered with, including by unlawful surveillance, unlawful entry, arbitrary evictions, etc.

Respect for correspondence

Everyone has the right to uninterrupted and uncensored communication with others – a right particularly of relevance in relation to phone-tapping; email surveillance; and the reading of letters.

Limitations

Article 8 is a qualified right and as such the right to a private and family life and respect for the home and correspondence may be limited. So while the right to privacy is engaged in a wide number of situations, the right may be lawfully limited. Any limitation must have regard to the fair balance that has to be struck between the competing interests of the individual and of the community as a whole.

In particular any limitation must be:

⇨ in accordance with law;

⇨ necessary and proportionate; and

⇨ for one or more of the following legitimate aims:

  ⇨ the interests of national security;

  ⇨ the interests of public safety or the economic well-being of the country;

  ⇨ the prevention of disorder or crime;

  ⇨ the protection of health or morals; or

  ⇨ the protection of the rights and freedoms of others.

Balancing rights

The right to respect for a private life often needs to be balanced against the right to freedom of expression. For example a public figure does not necessarily enjoy the same respect for their private life as others, as matters of public concern might justify the publication of information about that person that might otherwise interfere with the right to privacy.

⇨ The above information is reprinted with kind permission from Liberty. Please visit www.liberty-human-rights.org.uk for further information.

© Liberty 2013

The invention of privacy

From data to people.

Taking a long-range historical view, privacy is a relatively recent concept. It goes back only about 400 years. The first layer of privacy was controlled through architecture (the 'bricks and walls' layer). The second was controlled through legislation and laws (the 'paper' layer). And the third – and newest – layer is privacy controlled through digital technology (the 'code' layer). It may seem odd to talk about bricks in the digital age, but the insight from that era, when the idea of privacy was constructed, has important resonances today.

The 'bricks and walls' layer of privacy

Ideas about privacy have evolved in response to technology

The notion of privacy first emerged in Britain during the 16th century as a result of changes in the design of the home. Before then, the majority of homes had consisted of a single shared space where family and household members slept, cooked, ate and worked together. This changed between 1570 and 1640 following the invention of the chimney, which meant that homes no longer needed to be constructed around an open fire; instead houses could be divided into smaller rooms separated by walls. The result was a construction boom in Britain that became known as the 'Great Rebuilding'. People began adding floors, walls and stairs into their homes, creating smaller, separate rooms, each with its own special purpose. The home became divided into public rooms such as the living room and private rooms such as the bedroom.

Privacy: what you need to know

At the heart of the problem of online privacy are companies' attitudes towards data: at present the exchange of data between people and organisations is unbalanced and resembles a one-sided handshake.

Privacy as we know it is a relatively modern concept that was 'invented' around 400 years ago. Every time privacy has developed another layer of meaning, it has been in response to the introduction of a new technology into people's lives – from the chimney, to the camera and printing press, to the Internet. The future of privacy will be characterised by the analysis of patterns of consumers' behavioural data, with consumers seeking to protect themselves from the assumptions companies have made about their personal data patterns.

Privacy controversies most often happen because consumers are surprised when their personal data is used unexpectedly; companies need a 'no-surprises' approach to privacy if they want to avoid privacy pitfalls. In order to ensure there are no surprises around privacy we need to move the debate away from privacy as a permanent and immovable 'right', and recognise it for what it is in the

digital age: a mediating factor in a constantly shifting and iterative exchange between people and organisations. Until companies stop viewing personal data – or 'bits of people' – as a commodity to be farmed, and rather realise its role in an exchange which should be beneficial to both parties, they will fail to handle it with the care and respect consumers expect.

As long as this 'one-sided handshake' continues, companies and organisations that manage personal data not only risk a collapse in consumer trust, they also stand to miss out on huge potential sources of value to their business and society as a whole, from new unexpected uses of personal data co-created by their customers.

Two American lawyers invented the idea of the 'right to be left alone' after Eastman Kodak marketed the portable camera.

These changes in home design happened rapidly, as demonstrated by an inventory survey[1] conducted in the East Midlands from that period; in the 16th century the average number of rooms in a house was 2.5; by the 17th century this had increased to 6.5 rooms. It is unclear whether the desire for privacy led to the architectural reconfiguration of homes or the other way around. What is certain, though, is that the Great Rebuilding filtered concepts of privacy down to the broad population, with the creation of personal living spaces giving people a sense of individual privacy that had previously been experienced only by the rich.

That the home as a private space now seems normal and unremarkable exposes one assumption often made about privacy – that it has always been valued. Far from it: privacy is a relatively modern invention that was enabled by changes in our material conditions and surroundings. But as time elapsed, bricks and walls were no longer enough to protect personal privacy.

The 'paper' layer of privacy

This next layer of privacy was expressed and controlled through law. In 1890, the eminent American lawyers Samuel D. Warren and Louis Brandeis published an article in *The Harvard Law Review* which gave birth to the recognition of privacy as an individual right to be protected by law. As chimneys led to the notion of privacy through the physical architecture of the home, it was the invention of the camera that motivated the campaign for the 'right to privacy'.

The invention of the inexpensive and portable 'snap camera' by Eastman Kodak a few years before had created a new threat to privacy; individuals could now be photographed at home, at work or at play and the results published in

1 16th Century Inventory survey.
Orlin, Lena (2007), Locating Privacy in Tudor London, Oxford: OUP

newspapers for all to see. The motivation for the lawyers[2] to write their article apparently stemmed from their irritation at photos of Warren's dinner parties appearing in a Boston high-society gossip magazine.

In their article, Warren and Brandeis noted that the common law in America was primarily about the protection of the physical person and individual property. However, they went on to argue that the threat to privacy from recent technological inventions and the new forms of publicity associated with the development of the modern press meant that the common law needed to be extended to protect privacy. This eventually came to be known as 'the right to be left alone'.

The 'code' layer of privacy

In turn, the third and most recent layer of privacy, as code is intimately associated with online digital technologies. Technologies ranging from cookies on websites to GPS sensors on smartphones mean new types of data about people's behaviours can be easily collected on a mass scale. As a result of the Web, information that used to be forgettable simply because it was harder to find is now more easily circulated, stored and retrieved. In short, the Internet's memory is a lot better than the human memory: the Internet never forgets. To describe the current phase of privacy as that of 'code' points to what makes digital technologies unique – namely that they are underpinned by binary codes that convert real world information into discrete data formed of 0s and 1s. As Cory Doctorow has recently described in MIT's *Technology Review,*[3] there are currently only two ways to browse the Web. Either you turn off cookies (the bits of code used to track online behaviour) and live with the fact that many websites won't work, or you turn on all cookies and accept that this gives companies wholesale permission to extract the data collected by the cookies. Your privacy settings are, in other words, either on or off. This goes against the way people actually want to control their privacy, which is 'on' in some contexts (e.g. using a social network while at work) and 'off' in other contexts (e.g. using a social network while at home).

There are signs that a more contextually sensitive approach to privacy is emerging. For example, Google Circles

2 Wacks, Raymond (2010). Privacy: A very short introduction. OUP: Oxford

provides a more layered way of controlling who gets to see what on a social network. However, the code layer is still in the process of developing. Emerging technologies such as the Internet of Things (where objects such as fridges, cars and light bulbs are embedded with computational capabilities) will push the code layer of privacy further; privacy will no longer be about only the data collected and stored on devices like mobile phones and computers but also about the data collected by seemingly innocuous household objects.

Competing world views on privacy

Great Britain

Britain has one of the oldest histories of privacy and as a result privacy is engrained within law and society. As

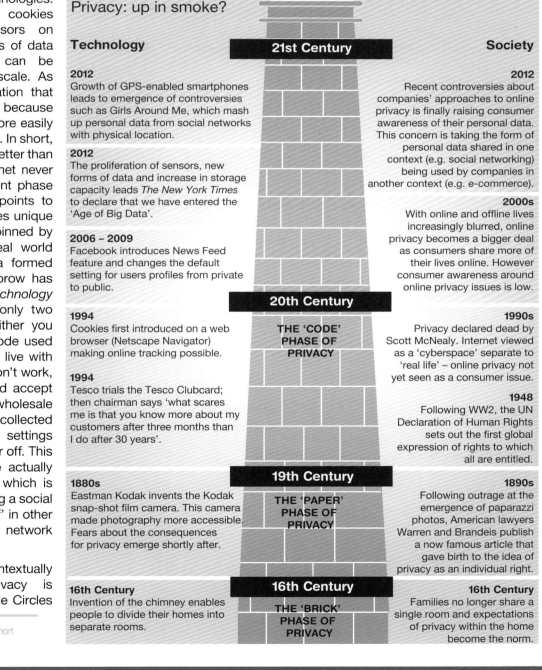

Privacy: up in smoke?

Technology

21st Century

2012
Growth of GPS-enabled smartphones leads to emergence of controversies such as Girls Around Me, which mash up personal data from social networks with physical location.

2012
The proliferation of sensors, new forms of data and increase in storage capacity leads *The New York Times* to declare that we have entered the 'Age of Big Data'.

2006 – 2009
Facebook introduces News Feed feature and changes the default setting for users profiles from private to public.

20th Century

THE 'CODE' PHASE OF PRIVACY

1994
Cookies first introduced on a web browser (Netscape Navigator) making online tracking possible.

1994
Tesco trials the Tesco Clubcard; then chairman says 'what scares me is that you know more about my customers after three months than I do after 30 years'.

19th Century

THE 'PAPER' PHASE OF PRIVACY

1880s
Eastman Kodak invents the Kodak snap-shot film camera. This camera made photography more accessible. Fears about the consequences for privacy emerge shortly after.

16th Century
Invention of the chimney enables people to divide their homes into separate rooms.

16th Century

THE 'BRICK' PHASE OF PRIVACY

Society

2012
Recent controversies about companies' approaches to online privacy is finally raising consumer awareness of their personal data. This concern is taking the form of personal data shared in one context (e.g. social networking) being used by companies in another context (e.g. e-commerce).

2000s
With online and offline lives increasingly blurred, online privacy becomes a bigger deal as consumers share more of their lives online. However consumer awareness around online privacy issues is low.

1990s
Privacy declared dead by Scott McNealy. Internet viewed as a 'cyberspace' separate to 'real life' – online privacy not yet seen as a consumer issue.

1948
Following WW2, the UN Declaration of Human Rights sets out the first global expression of rights to which all are entitled.

1890s
Following outrage at the emergence of paparazzi photos, American lawyers Warren and Brandeis publish a now famous article that gave birth to the idea of privacy as an individual right.

16th Century
Families no longer share a single room and expectations of privacy within the home become the norm.

such, privacy breaches are met with particularly vehement opposition.

Germany

Since atrocities in the Second World War, privacy has been deeply embedded in German law. Germany is a campaigner for stricter regulations globally.

Russia

The Russian constitution guarantees a broad right to privacy; however, Russia lacks the tailored judicial procedures to enforce its complex privacy rules.

USA

Privacy is not acknowledged explicitly in the constitution. Increasingly there is tension between freedom of expression, one of the most prominent amendments of their constitution, and the right to privacy, a human right that has been adopted into the law more recently.

Brazil

The Brazilian constitution describes privacy as 'inviolable' and guarantees money for some breaches. However, Brazil has no specific comprehensive data privacy law in place.

South Africa

Data protection and privacy are separate in law but closely linked. Privacy is listed as a constitutional human right.

India

India's supreme court incorporates privacy into a larger Indian right to 'social liberty'.

China

The Chinese constitution only provides limited rights to privacy because the rights are subject to broad exemptions with the view to protecting the security of the country.

As the layers of privacy become thicker over time, legal institutions across the world have adapted different ways to keep up with the shifting privacy landscape. Political history, cultural sensitivity and economic prosperity all play a part in the ways that privacy is adapted into constitutions and law.

⇨ The above information is reprinted with kind permission from The Futures Company. Please visit www. thefuturescompany.com for further information.

Data protection and privacy laws

Effective legislation helps minimise monitoring by governments, regulate surveillance by companies and ensure that personal information is properly protected.

Laws for the protection of privacy have been adopted worldwide. Their objectives vary: some have attempted to remedy past injustices under authoritarian regimes, others seek to promote electronic commerce, and many ensure compliance with pan-European laws and to enable global trade. Regardless of the objective, data protection laws tend to converge around the principle that individuals should have control over their personal information.

Interest in the right to privacy increased in the 1960s and 1970s with the advent of information technology. The surveillance potential of powerful computer systems prompted demands for specific rules governing the collection and handling of personal information. The genesis of modern legislation in this area can be traced to the first data protection law in the world, enacted in the Land of Hesse in Germany in 1970. This was followed by national laws in Sweden (1973), the United States (1974), Germany (1977) and France (1978).

Two crucial international instruments evolved from these laws: the Council of Europe's 1981 Convention for the Protection of Individuals with regard to the Automatic Processing of Personal Data, and the Organisation for Economic Cooperation and Development's 1980 'Guidelines on the Protection of Privacy and Transborder Flows of Personal Data'. These rules describe personal information as data that are afforded protection at every step, from collection to storage and dissemination.

Although the expression of data protection requirements varies across jurisdictions, all require that personal information must be:

⇨ obtained fairly and lawfully

⇨ used only for the original specified purpose

⇨ adequate, relevant and not excessive to purpose

⇨ accurate and up to date

⇨ accessible to the subject

⇨ kept secure

⇨ destroyed after its purpose is completed.

⇨ The above information is reprinted with kind permission from Privacy International. Please visit www. privacyinternational.org for further information.

Communications Data Bill published

Vital powers to help catch criminals, save lives and protect children are outlined in the Communications Data Bill.

Communications data is information generated about a communication. It includes the time and duration of a communication, the number or email address of the originator and recipient and sometimes the location of the device from which the communication was made. Communications data is distinct from communications content.

The legislation will require Communications Service Providers, when requested to do so, to retain and store communications records which they may not retain at present for their own business reasons.

Communications data

Communications data is already used by the police and is vital for day-to-day police work and in particular the investigation of all forms of serious crime, including terrorism and child abuse. This legislation will ensure that, as communications technology changes, the police will maintain access to this data in future. But access to data will continue to be permitted only in the context of a specific investigation or operation.

Four key bodies will be allowed to apply for access to data under new rules in the Bill – the police, the Serious Organised Crime Agency (SOCA)/National Crime Agency (NCA), the intelligence agencies and Her Majesty's Revenue and Customs.

Hundreds of public bodies – including local authorities – currently have access to communications data, but will not be covered by the new laws unless Parliament agrees their use is vital to tackling crime and protecting the public.

Tackling crime and terrorism

The Bill will ensure law enforcement agencies maintain the ability to tackle crime and terrorism as criminals use modern technology and new ways of communicating to plan and commit crime. Without action by government crimes enabled by email and the Internet will increasingly go undetected and unpunished.

There has been a huge increase in the use of new technology and the volume of data on UK networks in recent years. There are now more than 80 million mobile phone subscriptions in the UK. Over a quarter of UK adults are smartphone users, with 60 per cent buying their phone in the last year. Data volumes transferred over mobile networks increased by 67 per cent in 2010.

Publishing the Bill today, Home Secretary Theresa May said: 'Communications data saves lives. It is a vital tool for the police to catch criminals and to protect children. If we stand by as technology changes we will leave police officers fighting crime with one hand tied behind their backs.

'Checking communication records, not content, is a crucial part of day-to-day policing and the fingerprinting of the modern age – we are determined to ensure its continued availability in cracking down on crime.'

New legislation will help ensure police can stay a step ahead of the criminals. But it will not:

⇨ enable unfettered access by the police to data about everyone's communications

⇨ provide the police and others with powers to intercept and read your emails, phone calls or check your contacts lists

⇨ create a single government database containing your emails and phone calls to which the police and agencies can get unlimited and unregulated access

⇨ weaken current safeguards or checks in place to protect communications data and allow local authorities greater powers.

Regulatory framework

The new proposals will see communications data taken out of the Regulation of Investigatory Powers Act (RIPA) and the creation of a new regulatory framework.

Access to the vast majority of communications data is currently conducted through RIPA, but there are a multitude of other powers public bodies can use – including Acts governing environmental protection, pensions and financial services.

The new Bill will replace the dozens of currently available powers with a single piece of legislation, all under the auspices of the Interception of Communications Commissioner.

The legislation will also ensure there is a level playing field for communication service providers (CSPs). They will be reimbursed for any costs of complying with legislation. Obligations will not be placed on every CSP and will only be imposed after detailed discussion and ministerial sign-off.

CSPs will be able to appeal to a technical advisory board under dispute procedures if they feel requests made of them are unnecessarily onerous.

Protecting the public

Association of Chief Police Officers (ACPO) crime head Jon Murphy, Chief Constable of Merseyside Police said: 'Communications data is vital to law enforcement. It is an essential and irreplaceable tool for protecting the public, keeping people safe from harm and, ultimately, saving lives.

'It provides investigative breakthroughs to the most serious of crimes, including child abuse, murder, rape, kidnapping, cyber crime and terrorism offences.'

CEOP Chief Executive Peter Davies said: 'We protect and safeguard children and pursue offenders who cause such serious harm. Without communications data and intelligence, we would not be able to act as fast as we need to and, in many instances, we would not be in a position to act at all.'

SOCA Director General Trevor Pearce said: 'Any significant reduction in the capability of law enforcement agencies to acquire and exploit intercept intelligence and evidential communications data would lead to more unsolved murders, more firearms on our streets, more successful robberies, more unresolved kidnaps, more harm from the use of class A drugs, more illegal immigration and more unsolved serious crime overall.

'This would mean SOCA, the Metropolitan Police Service and other agencies relying more heavily on more expensive, more risky and potentially more intrusive techniques to locate and apprehend offenders.'

14 June 2012

⇨ Information from the Home Office. Please visit www.homeoffice.gov. uk for further information.

Twitter, Virgin Media, O2 and ISPA slam data-snooping bill

The Joint Committee on the Government's Draft Communications Data Bill has published responses received by key industry players.

By Derek du Preez.

A number of companies, including Twitter and Virgin Media, have raised some serious concerns regarding the Government's Draft Communications Data Bill, which would give police access to communications data for the purposes of tackling serious crime.

Communications data includes information such as which websites individuals have visited, and who they have emailed, but not the actual content of exchanges. The Government wants to update existing data laws to enable police to access communications data generated by new technologies such as VoIP (voice over IP) service Skype.

The Draft Bill also plans to require communication service providers, when requested to do so, to retain and store communications records that they might not already keep.

Twitter has objected strongly to this requirement in particular, as it outlines that most government entities around the world have exerted great pressure on companies to minimise the collection of user data, rather than increase it.

The social media giant also claims that these requirements are likely to lead to it holding data on users outside the UK, which could create legal problems for the company.

Twitter said in a written statement to the Joint Committee on the Government's Draft Communication Bill: 'We would be interested to understand what consideration was given to issues of proportionality in the drafting of this provision as well as some cross jurisdictional challenges which may arise.

'For example, it is possible and indeed highly likely that this type of monitoring would result in the collection and retention of data on users who are outside the UK. This has the potential to place us in a legally untenable position with respect to privacy.'

O2 also criticised the Bill by saying that if it were required to collect any data that 'happens to traverse' over its network this will introduce 'expensive duplication, drastically reduce the usefulness of data collected and create a harsh commercial imbalance in the communications industry.'

Virgin Media also focused on data retention as its primary concern and claimed that widening the scope could impact its commercial relationships.

It said: 'Virgin Media currently enjoys good working relationships with a range of third parties, both domestically and internationally. In many cases, Virgin Media makes their applications and services available to its customers through, for example, its TiVo service.

'If Virgin Media is legally obliged to provide data from such third parties, this may well damage its commercial relationship with those parties and other third parties, particularly those based overseas.'

Finally, the UK's trade association for providers of Internet services, ISPA, issued one of the most damning statements, in which it said that the Bill has the potential to put the UK at a competitive disadvantage and destabilise the market. It said that it could make the UK a less attractive and more onerous place to do business digitally.

ISPA commented: 'Far too much discretion is given to the Home Secretary without the necessary parliamentary oversight to ensure that significant changes proposed are proportionate and necessary.

'Parliament should be told what data will be retained, for what purposes and make sure that the necessary safeguards are in place to balance the differing interests of law enforcement, users and businesses.'

All responses will now be examined by the parliamentary joint committee.

12 September 2012

⇨ The above information is reprinted with kind permission from ComputerworldUK. Please visit www.computerworlduk. com for further information.

Snoopers' Charter mythbuster

The Government is proposing the mass collection and storage of 'communications data' for the entire population. Here, we show why the most common arguments for these plans don't stand up to scrutiny. We are a nation of citizens, not suspects. Say NO to the snoopers' charter.

'If you've got nothing to hide, you've got nothing to fear'

Why is it always about what we've got to hide? What about what we have to protect – like a little bit of private space? Would you be happy if the police popped by tomorrow to install a CCTV camera in your living room just in case they one day suspect you have committed a crime? Crime prevention arguments must not unquestionably trump the privacy of law-abiding citizens.

'It's not about the content – reading people's emails or listening to their telephone calls. It's about the "who, when and where" of communications'

Your 'communications data' trail can build up a frighteningly detailed picture of your life: who you have texted, emailed and telephoned on any given day; where you were when the contact was made and for how long; which websites you have visited in the privacy of your own home and more. In particular, web addresses can tell you an awful lot about a person – the state of their health, their hobbies or political interests.

'The Communications Data Bill won't change anything. It's already a requirement for some texts, emails and phone calls to be stored'

This requirement is already problematic and the Government now wants to go much further. For the first time private companies will be instructed to collect information on billions of communications made by their customers for no other reason than the authorities' future demands for access. This amounts to mass, blanket surveillance of the population outsourced to the private sector.

For these reasons courts in Germany, Romania, Bulgaria, Cyprus and the Czech Republic have found similar arrangements in their respective countries to be unconstitutional.

'The police service needs access to this information to keep up with criminals and stop terrorists'

The police already have the power to put individuals they suspect of committing crime under surveillance. But this proposal will allow information to be collected about everyone, not just suspects.

And this is not just about serious crime or terrorism. Access to communications data is granted to local authorities and hundreds of other public bodies for a wide range of purposes that have nothing to do with crime fighting.

What's more there have and will always be methods of communication that do not come within the State's reach, ranging from the use of pay-as-you-go mobile phones to complicated encryption techniques. Whilst the data of many innocent people will be captured serious criminals will likely avoid detection.

'Communications companies and the state will keep our personal information safe and never look when they're not supposed to'

If the data loss scandals of recent years have taught us anything, it's that the building of huge and unwieldy databases carries real risks. In recent years the Government has lost 25 million child benefit records as well as the personal information of those serving in the armed forces, witnesses in criminal cases and prisoners. Local authorities have also used intrusive surveillance techniques to work out whether a family lived in the right school catchment area.

Building such a comprehensive database of the web habits of the whole population leaves us all at risk of bureaucratic error and even fraud.

'These proposals are a lot less serious than those proposed by the last Government because there won't be a central database'

Labour actually dropped plans for a central database very early on, so current proposals are more or less identical to the last Government's plans. We question the idea that contracting out data retention to the private sector offers more protection for our information or less intrusion into our private lives. Private companies have been responsible for a large number of data loss scandals in recent years and besides, it is surely not the role of big business to act as an arm of our law enforcement agencies.

⇨ The above information is reprinted with kind permission from Liberty. Please visit www.liberty-human-rights.org.uk for further information.

© Liberty 2013

Communications Data Bill survey

Half of the public think the Communications Data Bill is poor value for money and a strong majority say they do not trust that the data about Internet use will be kept secure, according to a YouGov survey commissioned by Big Brother Watch.

⇨ 50% of the public believe that the Government's draft Communications Data Bill is poor value for money. The Bill, which is currently being assessed by Parliament, would require companies to store details of UK Internet use for a year to be accessed by police and intelligence services. This includes details on who sends and receives messages on social media sites, the websites they visit and who they email but it does not include the content of the messages.

⇨ The Bill would be funded by public expenditure and is estimated to cost around £1.8 billion over ten years from 2012. Only one in eight people (12%) say the Bill is good value for money.

Insecurity of data

At present, the Bill proposes to give access of the data to the police, the Serious and Organised Crime Agency, the intelligence agencies and HM Revenue and Customs, with the potential to extend these powers to other bodies. Almost three-quarters (71%) of Britons say they do not trust that the data about Internet use will be kept secure, with less than one in five (19%) people rejecting this claim.

Internet usage

Although over four in ten (41%) people said they would be less likely to use online services and websites if they knew their activity was being recorded, almost half (48%) of Britons said this would make no difference.

Nick Pickles, Director of privacy and civil liberties campaign group Big Brother Watch, said: 'While the real criminals take simple steps to hide their activity, the law would require every single person's emails and messages to be monitored and the public are right to be concerned that the data won't be kept secure.'

Big Brother Watch is a campaign group that seeks to challenge policies that threaten privacy, freedoms and civil liberties, and to investigate the true scale of the surveillance state.

31 October 2012

⇨ The above information is reprinted with kind permission from YouGov. Please visit www.yougov.co.uk for further information.

© *2000–2013 YouGov plc*

In general, would you be more or less likely to use online services and websites if you knew that your activity was being recorded or would it make no difference?

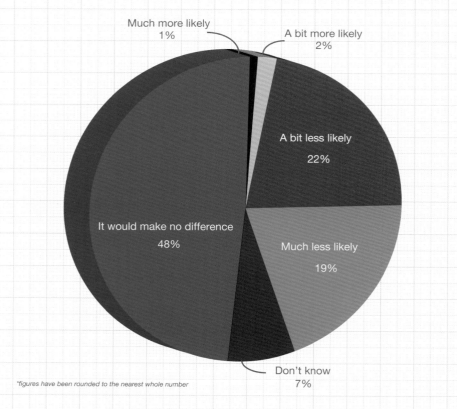

Much more likely 1%

A bit more likely 2%

A bit less likely 22%

It would make no difference 48%

Much less likely 19%

Don't know 7%

figures have been rounded to the nearest whole number

Source: YouGov/Big Brother Watch Survey Results, October 2012 © 2000–2013 YouGov plc.

Guidance on the rules on use of cookies and similar technologies

Privacy and electronic communications regulations.

The Privacy and Electronic Communications (EC Directive) Regulations 2003 (the Regulations) cover the use of cookies and similar technologies for storing information, and accessing information stored, on a user's equipment such as their computer or mobile.

A cookie is a small file, typically of letters and numbers, downloaded on to a device when the user accesses certain websites. Cookies are then sent back to originating website on each subsequent visit. Cookies are useful because they allow a website to recognise a user's device. The Regulations apply to cookies and also to similar technologies for storing information. This could include, for example, Local Shared Objects.

The use of cookies and similar technologies has for some time been commonplace and cookies in particular are important in the provision of many online services. Using such technologies is not, therefore, prohibited by the Regulations but they do require that people are told about cookies and given the choice as to which of their online activities are monitored in this way.

This guidance will explain how the rules apply for those operating websites and using cookies. The guidance uses the term 'cookies' to refer to cookies and similar technologies covered by the Regulations.

Background

The 2003 Regulations implemented a European Directive – 2002/58/EC – which is concerned with the protection of privacy in the electronic communications sector. In 2009 this Directive was amended by Directive 2009/136/EC. This included a change to Article 5(3) of the E-Privacy Directive requiring consent for storage or access to information stored on a subscriber or user's terminal equipment – in other words a requirement to obtain consent for cookies and similar technologies.

Governments in Europe had until 25 May 2011 to implement these changes into their own law. The UK introduced the amendments on 25 May 2011 through The Privacy and Electronic Communications (EC Directive) (Amendment) Regulations 2011.

The rules in this area are essentially designed to protect the privacy of Internet users – even where the information being collected about them is not directly personally identifiable. The changes to the Directive in 2009 were prompted in part by concerns about online tracking of individuals and the use of spyware. These are not rules designed to restrict the use of particular technologies as such, they are intended to prevent information being stored on people's computers, and used to recognise them via the device they are using, without their knowledge and agreement.

Consumer understanding of cookies

A clear understanding of users' levels of awareness of what cookies are, what they are used for and how they can be managed, is fundamental to any consideration of the level of detail that needs to be provided about cookies, and the way in which the requirement to obtain consent can be satisfied.

Research into consumers' understanding of the Internet and cookies demonstrates that current levels of awareness of the way cookies are used and the options available to manage them is limited. The Department for Culture, Media and Sport commissioned PricewaterhouseCoopers LLP (PWC) to conduct research into the potential impact of cookies regulation. PWC conducted an online survey of over 1,000 individuals in February 2011. Despite the report acknowledging that the most intensive Internet users are overrepresented in the sample, the results illustrate that significant percentages of these more 'Internet savvy' consumers have limited understanding of cookies and how to manage them:

⇨ 41% of those surveyed were unaware of any of the different types of cookies (first party, third party, Flash/Local Storage). Only 50% were aware of first party cookies.

⇨ Only 13% of respondents indicated that they fully understood how cookies work, 37% had heard of Internet cookies but did not understand how they work and 2% of people had not heard of Internet cookies before participating in the survey.

⇨ 37% said they did not know how to manage cookies on their computer.

> **A cookie is a small file, typically of letters and numbers, downloaded on to a device when the user accesses certain websites. Cookies are then sent back to the originating website on each subsequent visit.**

⇨ The survey tested respondents' knowledge of cookies, asking them to confirm if a number of statements about cookies were correct or not. Out of the 16 statements only one was answered correctly by the majority of respondents.

"Broader education about online privacy could go a long way toward making users feel more comfortable online"

Those who use the Internet less regularly, or have a generally lower level of technical awareness, are even less likely to understand the way cookies work and how to manage them. The report concluded that 'broader consumer education about basic online privacy fundamentals could go a long way toward making users feel more comfortable online and also enable them to take more control of their privacy while online' and that 'online businesses will need to evolve their data collection and usage transparency in order to illustrate to consumers the benefits of opting-in'.

May 2012

⇨ The above information is an extract from the Information Commissioner's Office *Privacy and Electronic Communications Regulations: Guidance on the rules on use of cookies and similar technologies*, and is reproduced with permission. Please visit www.ico.gov.uk for further information.

© *Information Commissioner's Office 2012*

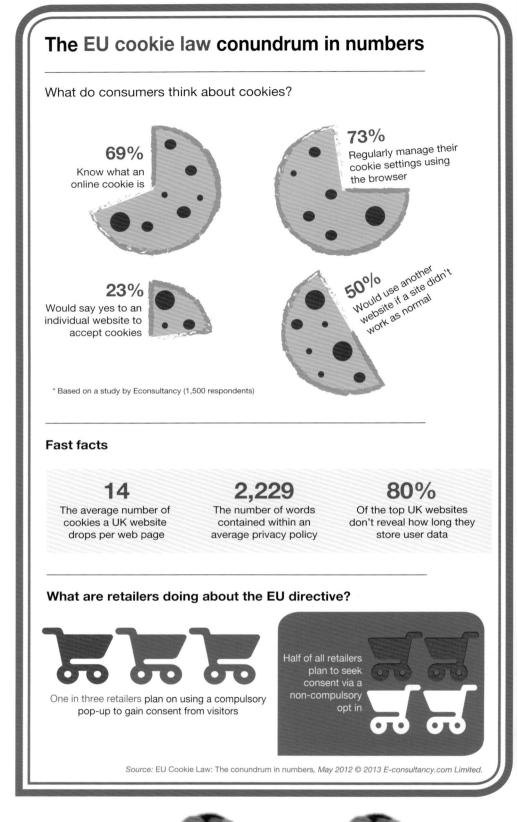

The EU cookie law conundrum in numbers

What do consumers think about cookies?

69%
Know what an online cookie is

73%
Regularly manage their cookie settings using the browser

23%
Would say yes to an individual website to accept cookies

50%
Would use another website if a site didn't work as normal

* Based on a study by Econsultancy (1,500 respondents)

Fast facts

14
The average number of cookies a UK website drops per web page

2,229
The number of words contained within an average privacy policy

80%
Of the top UK websites don't reveal how long they store user data

What are retailers doing about the EU directive?

One in three retailers plan on using a compulsory pop-up to gain consent from visitors

Half of all retailers plan to seek consent via a non-compulsory opt in

Source: EU Cookie Law: The conundrum in numbers, May 2012 © 2013 E-consultancy.com Limited.

The Data Protection Act

The Data Protection Act controls how your personal information is used by organisations, businesses or the Government.

Everyone who is responsible for using data has to follow strict rules called 'data protection principles'. They must make sure the information is:

⇨ used fairly and lawfully

⇨ used for limited, specifically stated purposes

⇨ used in a way that is adequate, relevant and not excessive

⇨ accurate

⇨ kept for no longer than is absolutely necessary

⇨ handled according to people's data protection rights

⇨ kept safe and secure

⇨ not transferred outside the UK without adequate protection.

There is stronger legal protection for more sensitive information, such as:

⇨ ethnic background

⇨ political opinions

⇨ religious beliefs

⇨ health

⇨ sexual health

⇨ criminal records.

Find out what data an organisation has about you

The Data Protection Act gives you the right to find out what information the Government and other organisations stores about you.

Write to the organisation and ask for a copy of the information they hold about you. If you do not know who in the organisation to write to, address your letter to the company secretary.

The organisation is legally required to provide you with a copy of the information they hold about you if you request it.

When information can be withheld

There are some situations when organisations are allowed to withhold information, e.g. if the information is about:

⇨ the prevention, detection or investigation of a crime

⇨ national security or the armed forces

⇨ the assessment or collection of tax

⇨ judicial or ministerial appointments.

An organisation doesn't have to say why they are withholding information.

How much it costs

Some organisations may charge you for providing the information. The cost is usually no more than £10 but it can be more if the information is contained within either:

⇨ certain types of records, e.g. health or education records

⇨ a large number of paper records held in an unstructured way by a public authority.

⇨ The above information is reprinted with kind permission from GOV.UK. Please visit www.gov.uk for further information.

© Crown Copyright 2013

The big debate: open data

From education to policing, from health to councils – public leaders tell us how they are tackling the challenge of making information available to citizens.

By Mark Smith

The Commons public accounts committee recently slammed the Government's open data policy for releasing too much unintelligible raw data. But releasing more government data is a cornerstone of Government policy.

The open data white paper, published in June, states: 'From the prime minister down, central government is committed to making open data an effective engine of economic growth, social wellbeing, political accountability and public service improvement.'

How is this being translated across different public services? We asked public leaders how they are tackling the challenges, and reaping the potential benefits, of making more information available.

Councillor Nigel Murphy – Manchester city council; lead member for Digital Manchester and executive member for environment

Manchester is embarking on an ambitious challenge to become an open data-friendly city. The UK has lagged behind cities such as New York in releasing and promoting its open data, but now we're seeing public sector bodies begin to realise the importance of open data and how it could benefit residents.

Manchester City Council, like most public bodies, has some of its data openly available, but nowhere near enough. This has been partly due to non-engagement with the digital community about what creative use of apparently dry data can achieve.

Now we are talking to the community and working with partners to give them the data they need to help develop useful mobile and web apps and visualisations that will take Manchester up the digital leagues. This is not just about giving the digital playground something to do, but also driving genuine interest from residents.

A first Hackathon organised by the council and its partners is likely to take place later this year, followed by bigger events in 2013. It's vital that this is not a one-off event. With legacy a buzzword around the country at the moment, the same applies to releasing open data and the encouraging the developer community to pick it up, run with it, develop prototypes and then pass the baton, so they can be developed further at the next events.

Carole Willis – chief scientific adviser, Department for Education

We published the new-look school performance tables in December 2011/January 2012, giving parents more information than ever before about how their child's school is performing. In particular, we added 400% more data about secondary schools than in 2010.

In one easily accessible website, the performance tables help parents to compare schools at the same stage of education, providing key information needed to support choice. Parents can find out the school type and size, pupil and staff characteristics, and test and exam results for the main Key Stages. There is also information on school finances; for example, spending on teaching staff.

This information, part of the Government's drive for greater transparency, can help ensure that schools are held to account for the performance of all their pupils. The site has received more than 7.8 million hits since they were first published last December, and we are expecting another peak in the autumn as parents use the site to inform the school admissions process.

Simon Parr – chief constable, Cambridgeshire Constabulary

The public has a right to access information about policing in their area and my stance is that we as a service need to be as open and transparent as possible. The challenge comes in organising that data in a way that is easily digestible for the masses.

Holding back data protects no one and I would much rather allow the public access to too much information in a disorganised manner, than withhold information and provide the minimum in an organised way.

The nature of our work means that things are constantly changing and data collated one month can significantly change the next but it's important we share wherever possible. We have a well-established email scheme, e-cops, where local policing teams keep the public up to date on what is happening in their area.

The evolution of social media is also presenting us with opportunities to engage and share information with thousands of people and this is an area I am keen to explore further, as we scratch the surface and discover the opportunities that are out there.

Tim Kelsey – national director for patients and information, NHS Commissioning Board

Opening up health and care data is key to improving the outcomes and effectiveness of the NHS. Transparency is the hallmark of a modern, 21st-century citizen-centred health service. It empowers accountability and choice and transforms patient and public participation – individually and communally. Transparency is a fundamental tool for healthcare professionals to drive clinical quality and research.

The NHS is committed to being open and transparent about health and social care data. We publish more data than any other system in the world from cancer profiles for GP practices in England to patient complaints for individual NHS Trusts. This is just the start.

There is a lot more data in the pipeline that will be made available over the coming months and years and we are working with a range of organisations to help ensure people have access to the necessary support so they can properly understand the data and make the best use out of it.

Evidence suggests that opening up data can have a positive effect in improving our care services, our health outcomes – and can save money. As one very powerful example of this, the Society for Cardiothoracic Surgery reported that mortality in coronary artery surgery had fallen by a fifth and in aortic valve replacement surgery by a third over five years, as a result of public reporting of outcomes by individual surgeons. Overall, savings outweighed the costs of data collection more than threefold.

Francis Maude – minister for the Cabinet Office

This is the most open Government in British history and we are leading the world on the transparency agenda. In June I published the open data white paper, explaining how making anonymised public sector data more accessible and more usable will benefit everyone.

We agree with the Commons public accounts committee that open data allows citizens to hold us to account, improve public services, and bolster innovation and growth. Everyone should have access to open data, and that's why we have just overhauled our data.gov.uk site to make it much easier for people to use the data we are releasing.

So far, we've published nearly 9,000 datasets across a wide range of areas including transport, crime and justice. Every dataset published is measured against the five-star scheme developed by Sir Tim Berners-Lee, inventor of the world wide web. The scheme scores the data on how easy it is to understand and use, keeping check on whether we are living up to our promise to make sure that the data provides tangible uses and benefits. Tim is also one of the co-directors for our new Open Data Institute, launching in the autumn, which will ensure we are making the most out of the new data we're publishing.

This agenda is here to stay and it's happening across the whole spectrum of government. Departments have published their own open data strategies with a clear timetable of what datasets people can expect to be released and when. The prize at stake – better public services and a more prosperous UK – is just too good to ignore.

20 August 2012

⇨ The above information is reprinted with kind permission from *The Guardian*. Please visit www.guardian.co.uk for further information.

Key facts from Google's Transparency Report, June - December 2012

Google often receives requests from governments and courts around the world to hand over user data:

- In the last six months of 2012, over 8,000 data requests were made in the United States.

- On average, some form of data was produced for 88% of requests from the United States.

- India made nearly double the amount of data requests than the UK.

- The UK made 1,458 requests – 70% of which resulted in some form of data being produced.

- Canada, Switzerland and Denmark made the least number of requests.

- The highest percentages of requests that resulted in some form of data being released, were from Singapore, Taiwan, the UK and the United States.

- Only 1% of requests in Russia were granted data release.

Source: Google Transparency Report. www.google.com/transparencyreport/

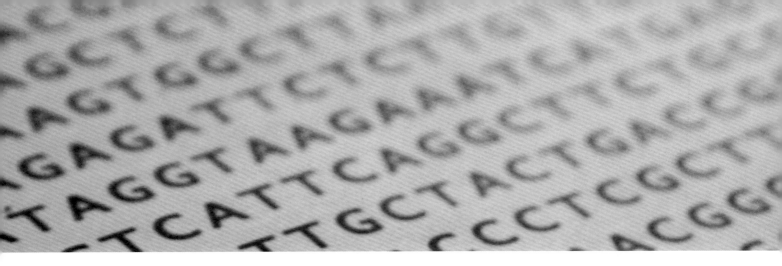

The National DNA Database

Between 1 April 2012 and 30 September 2012 the National DNA Database produced 61 matches to murder, 225 to rapes and 12,537 to other crime scenes.

The National DNA Database (NDNAD) continues to provide police with the most effective tool for the prevention and detection of crime since the development of fingerprint analysis over 100 years ago. Since 1998, more than 300,000 crimes have been detected with the aid of the Database, reassuring the public that offenders are more likely to be brought to justice.

Basic facts – FAQs

What is DNA?

Deoxyribonucleic acid, generally abbreviated as DNA, is a complex molecule found in virtually every cell of the human body and in all living organisms.

DNA carries the genetic instructions in the form of a code, used for the development and function of both cells and the organism as a whole and is the mechanism whereby this genetic information is passed from one generation to the next.

The vast majority of human DNA is exactly the same between individuals but small variations in the code are responsible for different physical characteristics such as height, eye colour, skin tone and hair colour, etc. Half our DNA is inherited from our mother and half from our father.

Non-identical siblings will inherit different combinations of DNA from the same parents and are therefore similar but different. Except for identical siblings, each person's DNA is unique.

Whose DNA is taken?

DNA samples are currently taken from anybody arrested for a recordable offence. Technically, recordable offences are those set out in the National Police Records (Recordable Offences) Regulations 2000 (S.I. 2000 No. 1139).

In practice they include any offence punishable with imprisonment and some additional offences specified in the schedule to the regulations.

People may be asked to provide DNA samples for elimination or volunteer purposes to assist an inquiry. These profiles will not be added to the NDNAD unless explicitly requested by the person providing the sample.

Perhaps the best way to get a feel for the severity of offences that are recordable is as follows – if you get stopped for speeding, it isn't a recordable offence and a DNA sample wouldn't be taken from you; if you get stopped for drink driving and are found to be over the limit, a DNA sample would be taken from you.

What is a DNA profile?

DNA profiling was discovered by Sir Alec Jeffreys during the 1980s. He discovered a way of distinguishing an individual's DNA: a biological identification system.

DNA profiling targets areas of the DNA that are known to differ widely between individuals. Apart from a gender test, these areas do not code for any physical characteristic or allow definitive determination of any medical condition.

The current system of DNA profiling used in the UK is known as SGM Plus. It examines ten sequence areas of DNA plus a gender test and produces a numeric DNA 'profile' which can be loaded electronically onto the NDNAD. This contains two numerical representations of the DNA at each area examined: one inherited from the mother and the other from the father.

When you look at a DNA profile held on the NDNAD, you will see it as a list of numbers, along with two letters (XX or XY) which show the result of the gender test. The number provides information about a feature of your DNA at each area we examine. For example, '11' informs us that at the particular sequence area of DNA examined, a very short sequence is repeated 11 times. When you see a '6', it means there are six repeats, and so on.

An example of an SGM Plus profile may look like this:

15,18; 6,9; 11,13; 22,22; 31,32.2;

14,17; 17,20; 11,12; 13,16.3; 15,16; XY

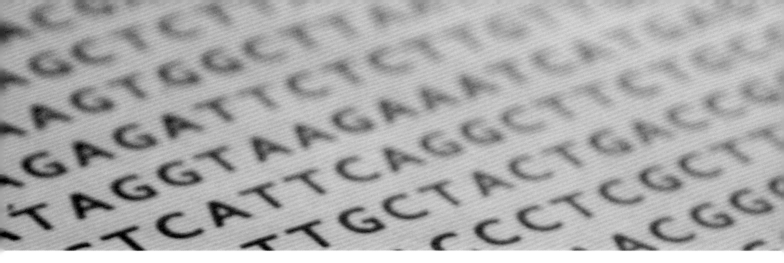

Although each person's DNA is unique (apart from identical siblings) DNA profiling does not examine all variations between individuals and therefore a DNA profile is not unique to an individual. It does, however, examine those areas of the DNA that discriminate widely between individuals and the chance of two unrelated individuals having matching full SGM Plus profiles is less than one in a billion (that is, a thousand million).

How many detections have resulted from DNA?

It is hard to say how many detections have resulted from the use of DNA as every case is different and other forms of evidence will also contribute to detections.

"There were over 410,000 crimes with DNA matches 1998 – 2008"

However, we are able to provide figures for the number of detected crimes in which a DNA match was available from profiles loaded to the NDNAD. In 2008/09, 17,607 crimes were detected in which a DNA match was available, including 70 'homicides' (this includes murder and manslaughter) and 168 rapes.

We also measure 'additional' detections which arise from the original case involving the DNA match. These happen where, for example, a suspect is presented with DNA evidence linking him to one crime and confesses to further offences. In 2008/09 there were 14,602 'additional' detections.

This brings the total number of crimes detected in 2008/09 in which a DNA match was available or played a part to 32,209.

We also measure the total number of DNA matches on the NDNAD, including those that do not result in a detection. A 'match' means that DNA found at a crime scene matches DNA from a person and includes cases that do not result in a detection, for example where someone has a legitimate reason for being at a crime scene. Even if there is no direct link to the offender, this can still be useful to the police, as it produces further information and speeds up the investigation.

There were over 410,000 crimes with DNA crime scene to person matches during the period 1998/99 to 2008/09.

⇨ The above information is reprinted with kind permission from National Policing Improvement Agency (NPIA). All information from the NPIA has now moved to www.gov.uk: search for 'the National DNA database'.

© Crown Copyright 2013

Case studies

Recent cases where DNA evidence was used

On 15 September 2011 Tobias Bruce burgled a property in Cranham Street, Jericho, Oxford. He was disturbed by the home owner after gaining access through an unsecured door. Tobias Bruce dropped an iPad and mobile phone when he was chased by the home owner. Police were able to obtain a DNA sample from the mobile phone keypad which was found to match a sample belonging to Tobias Bruce.

On 29 November 2011 Tobias Bruce burgled a property in Blackthorn Close, Headington, Oxford. He stole a laptop computer. Tobias Bruce's fingerprints were discovered on a window at the property. In February 2012 Tobias Bruce was found guilty of both burglaries; he also asked for a further six house burglaries to be taken into consideration. He was sentenced to 21 months imprisonment.

Innocent acquitted

Sean Hodgson (aka Robert Hodgson) was found guilty of the murder of Teresa de Simone in 1982. He had long pleaded his innocence after retracting his original statement. Sean Hodgson's case was urgently referred to court by the Criminal Cases Review Commission after his lawyers had insisted on DNA tests. These tests found that Sean Hodgson's DNA profile did not match the profile found at the crime scene. In 2009 senior judges ruled that Sean Hodgson's 1982 conviction was unsafe and should be quashed.

Eight million UK children on secret database without parental consent

One of the UK's largest government contractors has created a database which contains the personal details of eight million UK children, all without the knowledge or consent of their parents.

By Anne Sewell

The newly uncovered secret computer network, known as the 'One System', can apparently share children's personal information across different agencies in the United Kingdom.

According to *The Sunday Times*, the database was created by Capita, which is a company specialising in IT systems. Details of the information collected by the system includes the child's age, sex, examination results, bad behaviour including absenteeism, whether they have special needs and even how many minutes late they are to lessons.

This information can then reportedly be shared with various agencies, including the NHS, the police, charities and child protection units, all without parental knowledge or consent. It is apparently up to teachers to collect the data on all children, and not just those deemed to be a problem or at risk.

Nick Pickles from the privacy advocate group, Big Brother Watch, told the RT news channel, 'While information is absolutely essential to protect children, you need to collect information about children who are at risk and not every child.

'The only reason they've designed this is about profit, it's not about keeping children safe,' Pickles added.

Around two years ago, Contact Point, a similar database, was set up by the then-Labour Government, but was scrapped by the current Coalition due to security concerns. Now the One System is already employed by around 100 local authorities.

According to documents obtained by *The Sunday Times*, classroom information is gathered by teachers and then submitted to the One System up to six times a day. This is apparently to provide a 'golden thread of data', that can then be accessed by anyone working with children.

A further aspect of the system is that the firm hires photographers to take photos of the schoolchildren, which are then offered for sale to their parents, before they are uploaded onto the database.

Records of 48,000 pupils are already stored on the Capita One Database in Swindon, southern England, and have been shared with local NHS health officials and with teams working with young offenders.

The Sunday Times reports that according to Capita, this data could be used to identify vulnerable children who may need support from social workers, but Pickles disagrees. He said, 'Child protection cannot be delegated to an algorithm without local or individual knowledge of that child. Databases and computers remove human judgement.'

Pickles further argues that one of the main problems with the One System is the fact that it is not a centralised Government system, and is therefore not consistent across schools. He also expressed concern that data, once on a database, 'may be lost, stolen or misused'.

12 November 2012

⇨ The above information is reprinted with kind permission from Digital Journal. Please visit www.digitaljournal.com for further information.

Online personal data: the consumer perspective

Communications Consumer Panel research report.

Supplying personal data online

Three-quarters of the UK population now have broadband at home,[1] using the Internet to share their thoughts, ideas and information, and UK consumers conduct more transactions online, and are spending more, than consumers in any other major European country.[2] For them, providing personal data can have significant benefits in the form of services and applications that are more tailored to their needs, or that they might otherwise have to pay for. But there are also risks – that consumers disclose personal information without understanding how it is used or by whom, that data are misused, and that the law does not keep pace with industry developments or consumers' expectations.

A lack of trust and understanding among users could become a barrier to the continued development of innovative services and applications, and the benefits for consumers that they bring.

How concerned are consumers about data gathering? And what steps, if any, do they take to exercise control over the collection of their data?

Consumers' views

Against this backdrop, the Panel decided to carry out quantitative and qualitative research with consumers to understand:

⇨ the extent to which consumers are aware of the various methods of collecting data in the online environment;

⇨ the extent to which consumers are prepared to share their own data and what they expect in return;

⇨ consumer awareness of ways in which they can protect their online data, and their use of such methods;

⇨ among those using a social networking site, their use of privacy settings and understanding of how personal data on such sites can be accessed and used by third parties; and

⇨ attitudes towards what is currently being done to protect personal online data.

Just over half (52%) of UK Internet users have no top-of-mind concerns when using the Internet. The largest top-of-mind concern related to safety of personal details/ID theft – 26% of respondents said spontaneously that they were concerned about these issues, followed by 'privacy issues' (14%). When prompted, six in ten consumers said they were concerned about privacy online. Just over one in four of those who use the Internet on their mobile phone were more concerned about privacy when using their mobile phone than when using a PC, laptop or tablet.

Consumers can only take responsibility if they know how their data are being used online. There was a high level of awareness that companies collect customers' personal information by asking them to register details with them, and choosing to opt in or out of receiving marketing information (85%), but there was less awareness of passive methods used by companies to collect information. 64% of consumers were aware that cookies are used to collect data about the websites they visit; 59% were aware that companies can gather information from personal profiles on social networking websites (rising to 68% of Internet users with a social networking profile); and 45% were aware that mobile phone apps can also collect personal information. Awareness was higher among those who use the Internet on their mobile phone (53%).

"How concerned are consumers about data gathering?"

Consumers also need to understand the benefits of sharing their personal data. Otherwise they will not be able to make an informed decision between, on the one hand, withholding their data and protecting their privacy, and on the other hand, sharing their data and receiving benefits. The research findings suggest that the decisions consumers make might be influenced by how direct they perceive the benefits to be. Only a small minority of respondents were always happy for the methods of data collection we asked about to be used for any reason. In general, younger age groups were more relaxed about this. Respondents were slightly more comfortable if their data was collected as a result of registering with a company or by accepting cookies if this was from a company/brand they trusted. But neither receiving discounts/special offers nor relevant adverts/information increased people's comfort with these methods.

Levels of concern were lower if the personal information was being used by companies to develop new business and services (31%

1   http://www.ofcom.org.uk/static/marketdataresearch/statistics/main_set.pdf

2   See Ofcom's International Communications Market Report 2010 (ICMR), p217http://stakeholders.ofcom.org.uk/binaries/research/cmr/753567/icmr/ICMR_2010.pdf

had a high level of concern) than if it was being sold to third parties for them to target the consumer with products/services (here, 79% had a high level of concern).

"21% of people felt that it was solely their own responsibility to look after their data"

Respondents had relatively high levels of awareness of the types of methods that could be used to protect their information online, although those surveyed were more aware of reactive methods (e.g. opting out of marketing (83%) or reading a company's terms and conditions (78%)) rather than proactive means (e.g. blocking cookies (68%)) to protect their personal details. However, use of these methods varied significantly. Again, reactive methods were used much more – 73% of Internet users said they regularly opted out of receiving marketing/information from companies and 69% regularly opted out of sharing information with partner companies of the one they were interacting with. And looking at more proactive methods, 50% of respondents said they regularly read companies' privacy statements to inform their judgements, and 43% said they changed the cookies setting on their browser.

Those surveyed were more comfortable about their data being used when they had control over whether this happened, and knew how the data would be used.

Sharing financial information such as bank details, information from social networking sites and mobile numbers were the causes of most concern. Nearly nine in ten were highly concerned about providing, or companies being able to collect, credit card or debit card details.

The majority of social networking site users said they used privacy settings, and understood that if privacy settings are not set to 'private', anyone is able to access their information. However, 16% were not aware that information on open profiles could be seen by anyone, including companies, and 27% were not aware that this information could be used as the basis of targeted advertising. Nearly two-thirds (64%) of social network users said that they had a high level of concern about the use of information from profiles by companies.

While 12% of respondents felt that enough was currently being done to protect their information online, 22% were unaware of what was being done. 66% of Internet users felt more should be done to protect their personal information on the Internet.

21% of people felt that it was solely their own responsibility to look after their data, while 17% felt this responsibility should be shared with the companies collecting the information, the Government and an independent organisation.

The qualitative research explored participants' views about the provision of data to companies, both offline and online. When asked directly, people thought there was not much difference between the loyalty cards in shops and use of data online, but there was something about the human touch that made a difference. Personally handing over the card to someone seems to give people a greater sense of trust/control than online, where the exchange of data is happening in the background, often automatically and out of sight.

Participants in the research commented:

'It's basically the same, but with a card you actually get to speak to someone whereas on the Internet you give it to a server. But the information they collect is the same. I would say it was the same but I do prefer it when it comes from a person and not just through my laptop. There's nothing wrong with it happening online but it's just my opinion that I like the human touch.' (Male, 35–44 years old, Edinburgh)

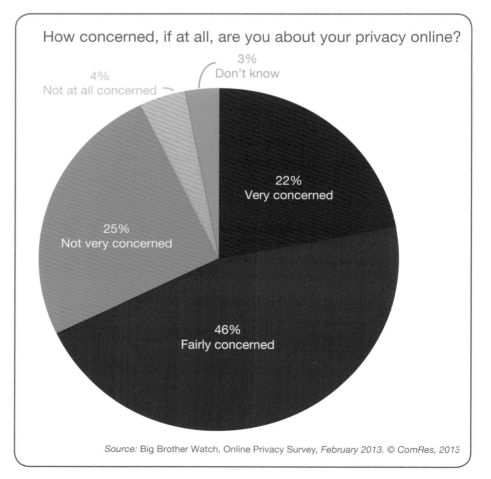

How concerned, if at all, are you about your privacy online?

3% Don't know

4% Not at all concerned

22% Very concerned

25% Not very concerned

46% Fairly concerned

Source: Big Brother Watch, Online Privacy Survey, February 2013. © ComRes, 2013

'I suppose realistically when you think about it they're the same. In fact the loyalty cards are probably worse because they collect more information about you. I haven't thought about it before but they are similar ... I tend not to think about how they use my information. I tend to think about how they use my information online more than through the cards though. That's because there's potentially more people who can access the information. I feel that with the card it should be protected better but I'm under no illusions, I know that that information is also stored on a computer somewhere.' (Male, 35–44 years old, Halifax)

The qualitative research also echoed the range of views found in the quantitative study:

'Normally when I am on these sites I won't click on the adverts to see what they are offering. But I am happy for them to use my information to tailor the ads.' (Female, 45–55 years old, Merseyside)

'It depends, if they are going to send me offers that I'll be interested in like discounts or new things that they have then it's better that they have my details so they can send them to me.' (Male, 16–24 years old, Leicester)

'I hate when you can't get to a certain page without opting in or registering. I don't like not knowing what they want my information for, especially if it is not a website that I am familiar with.' (Male, 35–44 years old, Edinburgh)

'I don't mind so much if one company has a piece of information but it's when they start joining it together that I don't like it. Even if they ask for your permission it's the principle that bothers me.' (Male, 35–44 years old, Birmingham)

'No, I didn't know about this. I don't think it is OK for companies to do this. If I haven't clicked an option then I don't want this to happen. There isn't really a reason why I don't want it, but if I was just minding my own business there is no reason for them to be targeting me with adverts.' (Male, 16–24 years old, Walsall)

Conclusions

The report is intended to inform policymakers, as they develop solutions, policies, and potential laws governing privacy, and to guide and motivate industry as it develops more robust and effective best practice and self-regulatory guidelines.

Consumers can only take responsibility if they know how their data are being collected and processed online. The Panel considers that companies should improve consumers' awareness of how their data are collected and used, and provide straightforward information for consumers.

In summary, the Panel considers that consumers will only be genuinely empowered if they have:

⇨ information to allow them to make an informed decision about the implications of releasing their data;

⇨ control over the use of their data;

⇨ reassurance that companies will always minimise the amount of data that they collect, store it securely, retain it for no longer than is necessary and consider whether to check with consumers after a set period of time whether they still wish their data to be retained; and

⇨ confidence that companies will follow the rules and manage personal data responsibly, and that if they do not, they will face robust enforcement action.

"I am happy for [sites] to use my information to tailor the ads"

The Panel looks forward to discussing with stakeholders how best to ensure that these conditions are fulfilled. In doing so, we want to ensure that consumers can make an informed decision about sharing their personal data online and maintain the levels of privacy with which they are comfortable.

May 2011

⇨ The above information is reprinted with kind permission from the Communications Consumer Panel. Please visit www.communications consumerpanel.org.uk for further information.

© Communications Consumer Panel 2011

Why you should be concerned about privacy online

Protecting your privacy online is vital to defend yourself against fraudsters, scammers, trolls and other threats when you're using the web. However, just how private you want to be, is up to you.

"Don't forget that what goes online tends to stay online"

Some people prefer to remain as anonymous as possible – the Internet is a very big place, and you never know who might be looking. Others prefer to simply limit the amount of information they share – for instance by controlling access to their personal details on social networking sites like Facebook so that only their friends can see them.

However much you decide to share, don't forget that what goes online tends to stay online. Once you've made public a message or a photo, it can be taken and used by someone, and perhaps posted somewhere else without your knowledge. Even if you take it down later, it could still pop up somewhere else. Those cheeky holiday photos may not damage your reputation now, but if it's possible that they might in the future, it's best to think twice about posting them. The Internet doesn't forget, so you should be sure that you're happy with anything you post online to remain there.

"The Internet is a very big place, and you never know who might be looking"

As usual with online safety, a few simple guidelines combined with common sense should be enough to protect you against most privacy issues.

Tips to protect your privacy

Don't post what you don't want others to know

The Internet never forgets and anything that you post online, whether you make it private or not, could become public later. So before posting any personal information online think about whether or not you would really want others to know it.

Keep personal information to yourself

Whether you're using the Internet for work or for fun, don't disclose personal information, such as your date of birth, address details, telephone numbers or holiday plans unless really necessary. Check your privacy settings on any social networks you use so that your personal information is only visible to the people you want it to be.

Use different email addresses

Keep your email addresses separate – so for example don't use your work email for personal messages and vice versa. Use a disposable, anonymous email account for websites that ask you to sign up – Google, Hotmail and others provide free email addresses.

Use security technology

Keep your computer secure with spyware or anti-virus software.

Control cookies

Learn how to turn cookies off and on as needed, so that no-one can build a profile on you to make fraud easier.

Use public WiFi access points with care

Anybody with a radio receiving device can tune in to what you are doing, so if you need to access your bank account, for example, make sure you use a secure WiFi access point with a password.

Consider encryption

You can encrypt your emails and browsing history just in case anyone is able to access them. Work emails may already be encrypted by your employer, but doing it at home usually means you'll have to pay for encryption software.

How to check what the Internet knows about you

The simplest way to find out what information about you is available about you on the Internet is to type your name into a search engine such as Google and see what comes up. All the big search engines allow you to refine your search, often including appearances on social networks and blogs.

"Common sense should be enough to protect you"

For a more in-depth enquiry, there are various websites which keep data profiles on people, gathered from many different sources, and make them available for a price. These sites might be referred to as people search, data brokers or info brokers and while they're technically legal, some have been the subject of privacy complaints.

⇨ The above information is reprinted with kind permission from Knowthenet. Please visit www.knowthenet.org.uk for further information.

© 2013 Knowthenet.org.uk

Careless generation

Careless generation are more concerned about their Facebook profile than falling victim to fraud, despite being an 'at risk' group.

Young people aged 18–25 are more likely to worry about the profile they share with their friends on social media than protecting themselves from becoming a victim of fraud, a new survey reveals.[1] While limiting who can see information on their profile is a key priority, young people feel that when it comes to fraud they simply aren't at risk, despite figures showing that this demographic admitted they were unsure whether they would recognise a fraudulent approach.

The survey which sees Government, banking and the telecoms industry join forces, forms the backbone of a new campaign entitled 'The Devil's in Your Details', designed to increase awareness amongst young people of the risks of becoming a victim of fraud.

Peter Wilson, Director, National Fraud Authority, says:

'Unsurprisingly, our research shows that young people are impulsive and naturally less risk adverse. However, what is concerning is that these underlying character traits are resulting in them being more careless with personal information, leaving them open to fraud.'

'Young people are much more concerned with managing what their friends see on social media sites such as Facebook. If they had the same level of concern when it came to protecting their personal details from fraudsters, their risk of being a victim would be significantly reduced.'

It is estimated that over £38 billion is lost within the UK to fraud, with £0.54 billion lost to online ticketing scams and bogus career opportunity offers – types of fraud young people aged 18–25 suffer from the most.[2,3]

Research findings found that for young people:

⇨ 73 per cent occasionally or never think about fraud

⇨ 59 per cent were unconcerned about being a victim of fraud

⇨ Whereas 82 per cent actively limit the information they share on social networks caring more about their image online than fraud.

Peter Wilson continues:

'Young people just don't think fraud will happen to them and if it does, many believe that someone else will simply pick up the cost.'

---

1 A pre-campaign survey was conducted by IPSOS Mori to benchmark awareness and behaviour. The survey was completed by online panel interviews with 500 women aged 35–55.

'Whereas other vulnerable groups such as the elderly are naturally cautious and take precautions against being a victim, young people's more carefree approach makes it harder for us to get the message through and influence them to do more to protect their personal information. This makes them a very high-risk group.'

"Young people just don't think fraud will happen to them and if it does, many believe that someone else will simply pick up the cost"

The Devil's in Your Details is a hard-hitting viral Facebook campaign, which has already gained an underground following on social networks. The application takes users names and profile pictures and puts them into a undercover video report. The campaign can be seen at www.thedevilsinyourdetails. com.

Working in partnership with Action Fraud – the UK's national fraud and Internet crime reporting and support centre, The Telecommunications UK Fraud Forum (TUFF) and Financial Fraud Action UK – the name under which the financial services industry co-ordinates its activity on fraud prevention, this campaign looks to raise awareness of the importance of protecting personal information and aims to educate this demographic on how they can keep themselves safe, by outlining what they should look out for when it comes to fraud and the methods fraudsters use to target them.

Peter Wilson concludes:

'This group needs to take action as they have more to lose than they realise. The time and effort needed to sort fraud out can be overwhelming. Aside from the hassle, fraud can even affect your credit rating, which could make taking out a loan or even a phone contract a complicated affair. Young people also forget that their social image, which this age group are evidently concerned about, could be under threat if a fraudster invades their network. The effects of which can be devastating.'

"The time and effort needed to sort fraud out can be overwhelming"

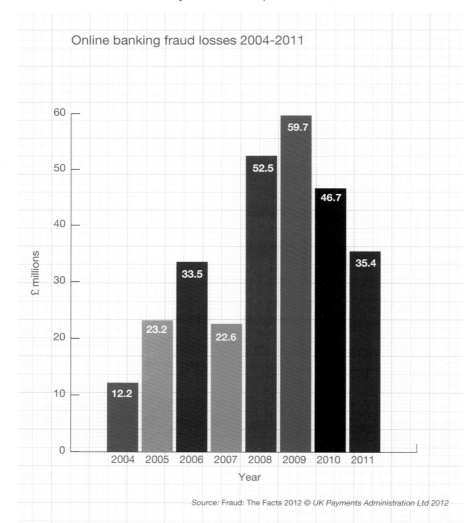

Online banking fraud losses 2004-2011

£ millions / Year

2004: 12.2
2005: 23.2
2006: 33.5
2007: 22.6
2008: 52.5
2009: 59.7
2010: 46.7
2011: 35.4

Source: Fraud: The Facts 2012 © UK Payments Administration Ltd 2012

Notes

The Devil's In Your Details Campaign

The National Fraud Authority (NFA)-backed campaign is raising awareness of the importance of protecting personal information and aims to educate the public on how they can keep themselves safe, by outlining what details should and shouldn't be shared over the phone, online and in person.

The Devil's In Your Details campaign encourages consumers to suspect anyone or anything they are uncertain about, to keep asking questions and to challenge or end an engagement if it feels uncomfortable.

As an introduction to a wider campaign against fraud, this initial awareness will work to increase the reporting of fraudulent incidents, in turn making it harder for criminals to conduct fraudulent crimes in the future.

14 March 2012

⇨   The above information is reprinted with kind permission from Action Fraud. Please visit www.actionfraud. police.uk for further information.

Facebook's Generation Y nightmare

Today's young people could pay a high price pay at work or in health insurance for giving up their privacy online.

By Frédéric Filloux

Taos, New Mexico, autumn 2012. At 18, Tina Porter has been on Facebook for four years

Duly briefed by her parents, a teacher and a therapist, she takes great care not to put contents – remarks on her wall, photos, videos – that could expose her in an unwanted manner.

Still, spending about 30 hours a month on the social network, she has become as transparent as a looking glass. It will impact the cost of her health insurance, her ability to get a loan and to find a job.

Denver, Colorado, spring 2018

Tina is now 24. She's finishing her law degree at Colorado State University. She's gone through a lot: experimenting with substances, been pulled over for speeding a couple of times, relying on pills to regain some sleep after being dumped by her boyfriend. While Tina had her share of downs, she also has her ups. Living in Denver she never missed an opportunity to go hiking, mountain biking, or skiing – except when she had to spend 48 gruesome hours in the dark, alone with a severe migraine. But she remains fit, and she likes to record her sports performances on health sites – all connected to Facebook – and compare with friends.

Seattle, winter 2020

In a meeting room overlooking the foggy Puget Sound, Alan Parsons, head of human resources at the Wilson, McKenzie & Whitman law firm holds his monthly review of the next important hires. Parsons is with Marcus Chen, a senior associate at Narrative Data Inc.; both are poring over a selection of CVs. Narrative Data was created in 2015 by a group of MIT graduates. Still headquartered in Cambridge, Massachusetts, the startup now helps hundreds of corporations pick the right talent.

Narrative Data doesn't track core competencies

The firm is more into character and personality analysis; it assesses ability to sustain stress, to make the right decision under pressure. To achieve this, Narrative Data is staffed with linguists, mathematicians, statisticians, psychologists, sociologists, neuroscientists. What they basically do is data-mining of the social Internet: blogs, forums, Twitter, and of course Facebook. Over the years, they've drawn a map of behaviours, based on language people use. Thanks to Narrative Data's algorithm, everyone aged above 20 can have his or her life unfolded like a gigantic electronic papyrus scroll. HR people and recruiters love it. So do insurance companies and banks.

Of course, in 2015 no one will be dumb enough to write on his Facebook wall something like: 'Gee, bad week ahead, I'm heading to my third chemotherapy session.' But Narrative Data is able to pinpoint anyone's health problems by weaving together language patterns. For instance, it pores over health forums where people talk, openly but anonymously, about their conditions. By analysing millions of words, Narrative Data has mapped what it calls Health Clusters, data aggregates that provide remarkable accuracy in revealing health conditions. The Cambridge company is even working on a black programme able to 'de-anonymise' health forum members thanks to language patterns cross-matching with Facebook pages. But the project raises too many privacy issues do be rolled out – yet.

Tina Porter's CV popped up thanks to LinkedIn Expert, the social network's high-end professional service

LinkedIn, too, developed its own technology to data-mine resumés for specific competences. Tina's research on trade disputes between Korea and the US caught everyone's interest at Wilson, McKenzie & Whitman. That's why her '3D Resumé' – a Narrative Data trademark – is on the top of the pile, that is displayed on a large screen in the meeting room.

Narrative Data's Marcus Chen does the pitch: 'Tina Porter, 26. She's what you need for the transpacific trade issues you just mentioned, Alan. Her dissertation speaks for itself, she even learned Korean...' He pauses.

'But?...' Asks the HR guy.

'She's afflicted with acute migraines. It occurs at least a couple of times a month. She's good at concealing it, but our data shows it could be a problem,' Chen says.

'How the hell do you know that?'

'Well, she falls into this particular Health Cluster. In her Facebook babbling, she sometimes refers to a spike in her olfactory sensitivity – a known precursor to a migraine crisis. In addition, each time, for a period of several days, we see a slight drop in the number of words she uses in her posts, her vocabulary shrinks a bit, and her tweets, usually sharp, become less frequent and more nebulous. That's an obvious pattern for people suffering from serious migraine. In addition, the Zeo Sleeping Manager website and the stress management site HeartMath – both now connected with Facebook – suggest she suffers from insomnia. In other words, Alan, we think you can't take Ms Porter in the firm. Our Predictive Workforce Expenditure Model shows that she will cost you at least 15% more in lost productivity.

Not to mention the patterns in her Facebook entries suggesting a 75% chance for her to become pregnant in the next 18 months, again according to our models.'

'Not exactly a disease from what I know. But OK, let's move on'.

I stop here. You might think I'm over the top with this little tale

... but the (hopefully) fictitious Narrative Data Inc. could be the offspring of existing large consumer research firms, combined to semantic and data-mining experts such as Recorded Future. This Gothenburg (Sweden)-based company – with a branch in... Cambridge, Massachusetts – provides real-time analysis of about 150,000 sources (news services, social networks, blogs, government websites). The firm takes pride in its ability to predict a vast array of events.

Regarding the 'de-anonymising' the web, two years ago in Paris, I met a mathematician working on pattern detection models. He focused on locating individuals simply through their mobile phone habits. Even if the person buys a phone with a fake ID and uses it with great care, based on past behaviour, his/her real ID will be recovered in a matter of weeks. (As for Facebook, it recently launched a snitching program aimed at getting rid of pseudonyms – cool.)

Expanding such capabilities

…is only a matter of refining algorithms, setting up the right data hoses and lining up the processing power required to deal with petabytes of unstructured data. Not an issue any more. Moore's Law is definitely on the inquisitors' side.

24 September 2012

⇨ The above information is reprinted with kind permission from *The Guardian*. Please visit www.guardian.co.uk for further information.

Facebook and you

By Alice Moran

One in five British Facebook users polled in our online survey is currently considering deactivating their account, our results show. Of those contemplating logging out for the last time, more than half are doing so because they're bored with the website's service, while over a third have revealed that they are concerned by intrusive privacy settings.

Even so, the site maintains popularity among those surveyed, with nearly a third of users logging on several times a day, with a similar amount visiting Facebook at least once daily.

20% of the 1,605 British Facebook users we asked are considering deactivating their account.

While nearly three quarters (74%) are happy to retain their account with the social networking website.

53% of those we polled who are considering deactivating their account say they are doing so because they are bored with its service.

38% say they find the site's privacy settings intrusive.

11% of those considering deactivation said that they preferred to use an alternative social network.

11% of those we spoke to also said that they were considering leaving the site because they currently spend too much time on it.

27% say they would like to spend less time on the website than they do and just 3% want to spend more time on it.

30% of the Facebook users we asked say that in general, they log on to the website several times a day, while the same amount visits the site at least once a day.

38% say they still log onto the site with the same regularity as they always have, and 25% say that they now log on more than they did when they first joined up.

However, almost half of the Facebook users we questioned (45%) say they spend less than an hour a week on Facebook and 37% say they log on less regularly than when they first registered.

US-based social networking phenomenon Facebook regularly faces criticism regarding privacy settings, and earlier this month, the website was forced to apologise for the way it introduced a new system that recognises users' faces. The social website admitted it should have done more to inform members about the launch of the new feature, which is intended to speed up the process of assigning a name to a photograph, known as 'tagging'. Some accused the site of intruding on users' privacy through its apparently new ability to identify people using nothing more than a photograph.

Facebook currently has 687 million users worldwide, and aims to attract one billion users in the next few years. However, according to Inside Facebook, which tracks the site's popularity, overall growth has been lower than normal for April and May of this year. The United States apparently lost nearly six million users and the number of users in the United Kingdom has reportedly decreased by more than 100,000 people.

The rise of micro-blogging website Twitter may also have played a part in these losses. According to our poll, three in ten Facebook users we spoke to also have a Twitter account, and more than one in ten (11%) are considering deactivating their Facebook account because they prefer an alternative social network.

22 June 2011

⇨ The above information is reprinted with kind permission from YouGov. Please visit www.yougov.co.uk for further information.

Children and online privacy survey

Young people's use of social technology and their attitudes toward Data Protection.

Executive summary

'The i in online' data provides a large population (4,116 in total) analysis on the behaviours and attitudes of young people toward online technology and privacy. Some headline statistics confirm our beliefs around such matters:

⇨ children and young people readily engage with online social media

⇨ sometimes they struggle with the policies that are supposed to be in place to protect them

⇨ they are aware of the need to protect their data, but are not always equipped to do so.

Our respondents were asked whether they engaged in any social networking activities themselves. In total 69% of our respondents said they did use social networking sites. There were some gender differences, with girls (72%) more likely to have a social networking profile than boys (65%).

The social network that is most popular is unsurprisingly Facebook, with 47% of respondents saying they had a Facebook profile. Again unsurprisingly the vast majority of secondary school respondents (88%) had Facebook profiles. However, we also had over a third

(39%) of young people of primary school age who said they had Facebook profiles. Girls are slightly more likely (50% in total) to have Facebook profiles than boys (43%).

The second most popular social networking activity was MSN, with 20% of respondents using it. Girls are more likely (26%) than boys (15%) to use MSN. Somewhat surprisingly it was almost as likely for a young person of primary school age (21%) to use MSN as someone of secondary school age (27%).

Boys are also more likely (56%) than girls (33%) to have an avatar, a virtual representation of themselves. However, there is little evidence to show that having an avatar results in different behaviours or attitudes toward data protection.

Our respondents were asked whether they had ever read a privacy policy. In total 40% of respondents had, meaning 60% of young people have not read the privacy policies of the web sites they use. This statistic differed little between young people of primary and secondary school age, but girls were more likely (44%) than boys (35%) to read a privacy policy. Boys are likely to have a more relaxed attitude toward data

and data sharing, although this is far from irresponsible with the vast majority still believing their data should only be seen by friends and family and parental consent was necessary in all scenarios presented about where their data might be exposed.

When those who had not read a policy were asked why not, there were a variety of responses. 32% said they didn't know what a privacy policy was, with 23% saying they didn't know where to find it. A quarter felt they were too complicated, and another quarter did not feel it important. Interestingly, more secondary school respondents (44%) felt they were too complicated, although more primary children didn't know what a privacy policy was (37%).

Those who had looked at privacy policies had divided opinions, with around half (51%) thinking they were easy to find and 57% understanding what was there. The vast majority (84%) looked at the policy because they thought it was an important thing to do. There was little statistical variation across the demographic groups for those who had looked at privacy policies.

So we had an interesting split in our population – those who do engage in privacy policies may understand what is presented and think they are important. However, the majority of our respondents hadn't seen a policy for a number of reasons. They were also asked what might be done to improve privacy policies and a large number of children said privacy policies should be made more simple with 'less words'.

However, it was also clear that our respondents felt that privacy on social networking was important, with the vast majority (85%) saying that social networks should have the strongest privacy settings by default and an even larger majority (94%) feeling that clear rules were needed to help with the removal of

Our Privacy Policy
Think of this as the 'tattoo' privacy policy: Anything embarrassing you post online in the heat of the moment will be there forever, long after you've moved on.
Agree? click   NEXT

CCTV images: exploding the myths

Many members have responded to my request for information about their systems to help explode some of the myths relating to public area CCTV, but even more responses would help increase the accuracy. At the time of writing we have statistics on over ten per cent (over 40) of the public area CCTV systems which also coincidentally covers an area which includes over ten per cent (over six million) of the population.

The results have been fascinating, and all are available on the website; however, a summary of them follows.

The number of public area CCTV cameras

The off-quoted myth that the number of public area CCTV cameras is 4.2 million was totally destroyed by the CCTV User Group member survey and by DCC Graeme Gerrard's survey of Cheshire extrapolated to the UK, with less than ten per cent variation by the two approaches.

So the FACT is there are approximately 35,000 town and city centre Public Area cameras and approximately 1.8 million public area cameras owned by other organisations. A far cry from the 4.2 million!

The public opinion of public area CCTV

Our independent public opinion survey carried out a year ago also exploded the myths about levels of public support for CCTV, and destroyed the myth that the public were worried about their privacy.

⇨ 90 per cent SUPPORT the use of public area CCTV

⇨ 82 per cent believe CCTV saves money and court time

⇨ 80 per cent believe public area CCTV DOES NOT infringe on their right to privacy

⇨ 76 per cent believe there are the right amount OR TOO FEW public area CCTV cameras

⇨ 71 per cent believe CCTV in public areas makes them feel safer and reduces crime

⇨ 70 per cent are against any removal of public area CCTV cameras

⇨ 61 per cent are against any reduction in monitoring.

The cost effectiveness of public area CCTV

The survey of CCTV User Group systems produced some interesting statistics in terms of the cost of CCTV per incident viewed. I stress these only include the cost of operating the CCTV system, and of course the police have other significant costs in terms of their forensic analysis of CCTV images. In August 2010 Her Majesty's Inspector of Constabulary's report tabulated the cost per detection of fingerprint analysis and DNA analysis for all police forces in England and Wales.

The cost of CCTV per incident is compared with the cost per detection for DNA and fingerprints:

	DNA	Fingerprints	Public area CCTV
Highest cost	£17,361	£12,654	£953
Average cost	£7,137	£4,617	£163
Lowest cost	£1,233	£1,069	£16

Even allowing for additional costs by the police, there appears a significant cost benefit in the use of public area CCTV.

The cost to the public of public area CCTV

How much does public area CCTV cost each member of the population in the authority area that pays for it? The figures might be as surprising as the cost per incident above! For a full picture we also look at the cost per hour of operation, and the cost per arrest witnessed in which CCTV was involved.

	Cost per population	Cost per hour of operation	Cost per arrest witnessed
Highest cost	£4.49	£91.32	£1,000
Average cost	£2.16	£38.32	£464
Lowest cost	£0.30	£4.26	£65

With an average cost of just over £2 per person per year (say £10 per family per year), it demonstrates incredible value for money for the feel-safe factor in town and city centres and in assisting in securing convictions.

At an average cost per hour for a whole year's operation of under £40 for an average 160 camera system, I simply can't see any more cost-effective means of providing 'the eyes on the street' in any other manner.

Public attitudes to CCTV 'have shifted' following August riots

New research claims that public support for CCTV surveillance has strengthened following the riots in the UK this summer, with one in three people (37 per cent) stating their support for its use in public spaces has now increased.

The independent public opinion survey, commissioned by surveillance systems specialist, Synectics, has also revealed that 76 per cent feel safer in public areas knowing that CCTV is in operation.

The majority (72 per cent) expressed that they would be worried if their local council reduced CCTV security in order to save money, with 62 per cent wanting to see more in their local area.

Azadar Shah, Managing Director at Synectics, subsidiary of UK-based Quadnetics Group, comments: 'In the past, there's undoubtedly been public apprehension about the use of CCTV, but the research indicates that people now recognise the positive role it can play within a community.

'Security camera footage played a high-profile role in the riots – helping Police identify and apprehend offenders – and this appears to have made a strong impact on public support for CCTV surveillance. In fact, nine out of ten people actively support the use of CCTV footage to identify rioters.'

In Bristol, one of the cities hit by rioters, 127 individuals were captured on camera, which led to 59 people being identified and charged.

Gordon McLanaghan, emergency control centre manager at Bristol City Council said: 'Without CCTV footage it would have been virtually impossible to identify the individuals involved in the riots and gather the

necessary evidence. In a crowd of 200 people it can be difficult to pinpoint individual actions but CCTV footage provided to the police can be replayed as many times as required to identify each individual responsible and therefore provide critical evidence for investigations.'

Synectics works with over 100 local authorities throughout the UK providing CCTV solutions, including Manchester, Sheffield and Bristol.

Azadar adds: 'Advances in security technology have enhanced data-sharing capabilities between local authorities and the police, so police can quickly access recorded camera footage for offender identification purposes. We work closely with local authorities and police forces to develop solutions, which allow immediate data transfer for crime investigation, without impeding usage of the surveillance system.'

About the research

Independent research was carried out by research specialist, ICM, investigating public attitudes to CCTV. It was commissioned by Synectics.

ICM interviewed a random sample of 2,027 adults aged 18+ from its online panel between 30 September

and 2 October 2011. Surveys were conducted across the country and the results have been weighted to the profile of all adults. ICM is a member of the British Polling Council and abides by its rules. www.icmresearch.com.

Key findings

⇨ One in three people (37%) said their support for CCTV had increased following the riots.

⇨ 94% support using CCTV to identify rioters.

⇨ 76% feel safer in public areas knowing that CCTV is in operation.

⇨ 62% would like to see more CCTV in their local area.

⇨ 72% would be worried if their local council reduced CCTV security in order to save money.

Autumn 2011

⇨ The above information is reprinted with kind permission from CCTV Image. Please visit www.cctvusergroup.com for further information.

Crowdsourcing crime prevention

In normal circumstances crime doesn't pay but in the case of the start-up InternetEyes, shoplifting is proving lucrative.

The company, based at the Pool Innovation Centre, has devised an ingenious way of crowdsourcing crime prevention and business is expanding.

The service provides live streaming of CCTV footage from stores and businesses throughout the UK and Europe to be watched by alert citizens in their homes.

If someone spots a thief or something suspicious, they press an alert that sends an email with a link to a video recording of the event to the business owner.

More than 8,000 subscribers each pay £1.99 a month to watch footage from more than 100 locations and collectively spot around 30 suspicious events each day.

If a thief is apprehended, the 'spotter' is awarded up to £250 for their vigilance.

The service is the idea of businessman Tony Morgan, 66, who took nearly five years and £100,000 to find the technical solution.

Mr Morgan, who runs a B&B in Dawlish, Devon, says he thought of the idea when listening to a radio programme on shoplifting.

'I thought, 'Why can't we link CCTV to people's homes where they could watch and detect crime?''

The ethos of InternetEyes is real-time pro-active crime prevention that extends the Neighbourhood Watch principle into the digital world.

'We're preventing crime,' Mr Morgan says. 'We have a sticker on the door of each participating business saying 'InternetEyes patrols this store; you are being remotely viewed'.

'CCTV has been around for a long time, but nobody thinks it's a deterrent, because it's never watched.

'Each subscriber is given only a ten-minute feed from each location to prevent viewers from gaining intelligence that could be used in a robbery.

'This is to stop anyone looking at a shop, seeing what time they cash up, what time they go to the bank – but if you see someone stealing, you get an extra five minutes.

'Subscribers don't know which shop they're watching. The chances of you recognising the shop are very remote.

'We're only about detecting crime. It's not a voyeuristic site. No one can watch CCTV of a shop unless they're more than 30 miles away, so the chance of them recognising anyone are very, very slim.'

The company has now expanded to employ six people and is considering moving into the international market, including negotiating a contract to launch a service in Russia.

At home, other sectors such as the prevention of animal rustling on farms and metal thefts from the railways are obvious candidates for expansion. They have even had an inquiry from the Bath diocese raising the issue of lead disappearing from church roofs.

30 November 2012

⇨ The above information is reprinted with kind permission from InternetEyes. Please visit www.interneteyes.co.uk for further information.

CCTV and Big Brother

By Bob Morgan, Former Met Police, Lib Dem campaigner, community worker and activist.

There are some in the UK who fear the increase in 'Big Brother' CCTV surveillance of UK citizens as they go about their lives. I think that the most obvious CCTV cameras – the ones in the street – do not represent any such threat because they are not being monitored much of the time and in fact don't do what most of us think they do – they do not help in reducing crime or making us safer.

I don't want to undermine the understandable caution many people feel when they hear about the latest gadgets aimed at stopping crime or preventing terrorism when it often involves more of us being watched by people we can't see. This is healthy as far as I am concerned – we do need to strike a balance between over-surveillance and actually making people safer. CCTV cameras can be misused and we should guard against it. What I object to is the 'big sell' that goes on around CCTV – that it is worth spending lots of money on because it makes people in the community feel safer from crime – and *actually* safer from crime – because in the end it does neither.

"Be concerned when you hear the 'great news' of CCTV control rooms being merged so that more cameras are watched by fewer people in some distant control room"

Research has shown that CCTV has very little effect on crime levels – at best it reduces car crime in some car parks – but has little or no effect elsewhere. In my experience CCTV is heralded as something that will make people both feel safe and actually safer but then once put in place it disappoints people as over and over again crimes occur in places with cameras (therefore it is not prevented) and the recorded images cannot be used – or are not used to solve the crime. Millions of pounds of taxpayer's money have been spent on cameras which simply do not deliver what we were promised.

After the recent riots there were calls for more CCTV cameras and better monitoring of them but the cameras in place did not prevent the rioting. For every image we see of the riots we should remind ourselves that the riots occurred and people's lives and property were endangered in spite of cameras.

The police will make use of camera images especially in the case of serious crimes – riots and terrorism and murders – but again this is evidence that the crimes did happen under the cameras. If we are happy to pay out millions of pounds to help the police investigate the small numbers of serious crimes then that's fine – but this is not what people are told when they are sold the cameras – they think it will actually stop them being murdered or their shop or house being torched by rioters.

"If we do have money to spend on crime prevention then we should spend less on CCTV and more on better lighting and other crime prevention techniques"

Be concerned when you hear the 'great news' of CCTV control rooms being merged so that more cameras are watched by fewer people in some distant control room. Besides the meticulous trawling of images and footage after a crime has happened, the main hope for our safety is that a human being will be watching the screen (amongst many screens) when our crime happens – the chances are increasingly against that happening the more screens you have. And in many cases (in my experience) some cameras are not even being monitored at all – they are not being displayed in the control room because there are two few screens. Operators will tend to watch the busy town centres rather than the cameras in the less 'interesting areas'.

I may well be criticised for possibly causing people to feel less safe because they thought the cameras would stop a crime happening to them – but I prefer to say what I am saying rather than even more people finding out for themselves through bitter experience. I don't doubt that CCTV remains a popular idea – especially with people who have not had to rely on it.

If we do have money to spend on crime prevention then we should spend less on CCTV and more on better lighting and other crime prevention techniques – because there is better evidence that this will prevent crime more effectively. Just remember – every time you see a crime recorded on CCTV in the news – remember that the cameras did not prevent it.

8 July 2012

⇨ The above information is reprinted with kind permission from *The Huffington Post*. Please visit www.huffingtonpost.co.uk for further information.

Surveillance camera code of practice consultation

This consultation sought views on the scope and clarity of a surveillance draft code of practice and its likely impact. It ran from 7 February until 21 March 2013.

Since the first town centre Closed Circuit Television (CCTV) system was installed in King's Lynn in 1987, there has been a proliferation in the use of CCTV and Automatic Number Plate Recognition (ANPR) systems operated in public places in England and Wales by both public and private bodies.

These systems are deployed for a range of purposes, and are generally welcomed as a reassuring presence and for keeping the public safe. Technological developments have increased the capability of surveillance camera systems. This has in turn increased the capability of system operators, the police and the criminal justice system to protect people and property, investigate incidents and bring crimes to justice. It has also increased the risk of interference with a citizen's right to privacy.

The public must have confidence that surveillance is appropriate and proportionate, and that those who operate the camera systems, or use the images and information they capture, demonstrate integrity in doing so, and can be held to account.

This is why the Coalition agreement for government includes a commitment to the further regulation of CCTV, which has now been enacted in legislation through the Protection of Freedoms Act 2012.

This legislation provides a regulatory framework which is intended to complement and be coherent with existing legislation, such as the Data Protection Act 1998, the Human Rights Act 1998 and the Regulation of Investigatory Powers Act 2000. Technological and professional innovation does not stand still, so we must ensure that any new regulation is appropriate both now and in the future.

Following engagement and consultation with a wide range of interested parties and the public, a draft code of practice has now been prepared for publication alongside this consultation document. The draft code is built upon 12 guiding principles, and for the first time introduces a philosophy of surveillance by consent.

The Government sees an important parallel with the well-established concept of policing by consent, which is based upon a presumption of transparency and accountability. This assures the integrity of police officers and staff as they exercise their powers on behalf of the public.

This consultation sought your views on the scope and clarity of the draft code and its likely impact, and also sought to ensure that proper consideration is given to the position of the three non-territorial police forces and the Serious Organised Crime Agency.

7 February 2013

⇨ The above information is reprinted with kind permission from the Home Office. Please visit www.gov.uk for further information.

State surveillance

State sanctioned surveillance against specific individuals takes place on a massive scale, using the broad and confusing framework created under the Regulation of Investigatory Powers Act 2000 (RIPA) which regulates the use of and access to surveillance by public bodies.

This involves five types of different surveillance:

1 Interception of communications – e.g. listening to telephone calls, reading letters and emails.

2 Intrusive surveillance – e.g. placing bugs and filming in private places.

3 Directed surveillance – e.g. filming and covertly monitoring specific people generally in public places.

4 Use of covert human intelligence sources – e.g. informants and undercover operatives.

5 Accessing communications data – e.g accessing the record (but not the content) of emails, telephone calls and websites visited.

Under RIPA hundreds of public bodies have access to the last three types of surveillance including over 470 local authorities. Surveillance can be authorised for a wide range of purposes which includes such vague purposes as preventing 'disorder' or collecting tax.

⇨ The above information is reprinted with kind permission from Liberty. Please visit www. liberty-human-rights.org.uk for further information.

What is biometrics?

Biometrics determines identity by measuring the physical characteristics or traits that make every human being unique.

Biometric devices can verify identity by recognising characteristics including fingerprints, finger veins, iris, retina, DNA, hand (palm), or face measurements. Behavioural biometrics or traits include a person's gait, voice, signature or keystrokes.

Biometrics can also be used to identify certain characteristics, such as age or gender, or to mimic movement. In this context biometrics is increasingly used for purposes such as advertising and gaming and is known as soft biometrics.

Why biometrics?

Biometric technology offers the most accurate and reliable form of identification known to man. Unlike other forms of identification, such as passwords, PINs and ID cards, the biological entities used for biometrics cannot be transferred, stolen or lost, so that only the right individuals can gain access to secure areas or critical assets at any time.

Accurate identification reduces exposure to the risk of terrorism and fraud, while taking care of more everyday concerns, such as staff time-keeping, cost control and personnel movement. Biometric technology is also proven to reduce the overheads associated with manual processing and hardware. Where biometrics replaces other forms of ID, such as key cards and fobs,

organisations can eliminate the costs of replacing and updating hardware altogether.

With fewer staff required to supervise and administer identification and access control, organisations can expect significant improvements in productivity and efficiency.

Can someone steal my identity using my biometric information?

When a person is initially enrolled using a biometric device, for example an iris camera, fingerprint reader, or finger vein scanner, an encrypted template is produced and held in a database to be used for matching each time the individual presents themselves for biometric identification. The database does not hold any images of the person's actual face, finger or eye, only the encrypted template.

This renders the possibility of someone replicating an individual's biometrics, extremely unlikely.

Are all biometric devices as reliable as each other?

The principle of all biometric technology is unique identification, but there are variances in reliability, measured by False Acceptance Rates and False Rejection Rates (FAR and FRR). Biometric devices that are intended for mass applications, for example those used in laptops and phones, typically have a higher FAR than those used in airports, where security is paramount.

All manufacturers should be able to give you an indication of their FAR and FRR.

Which biometric device shall I choose?

There are many different types of biometric device, suited to different organisations and environments. The biometric device that's right for you will depend on your particular reasons for considering implementation. For example, where security is the driver, an iris recognition camera or multispectral fingerprint reader may be the best solution, as both are high-end biometric technologies. In organisations where the driver is cost control however – a manufacturing plant for example – a lower-end fingerprint reader may be more suitable.

Are biometric devices expensive?

The cost of biometric technology varies depending on how the device measures biometric differentials, e.g. by fingerprint or iris recognition, and also how robust the manufacturer has made their particular device. For example, the fingerprint readers from ievo and Lumidigm are designed to work in areas of high humidity and harsh light and are unaffected by dirt or abrasions. Lower-end fingerprint readers that are intended for indoor use and/or in corporate contexts are more easily affected by changes in temperature, and dirt.

As a general rule, the more reliable the device, the more it is likely to cost, but even sophisticated readers, targeted at environments where security isn't the only consideration can be reasonably priced.

⇨ The above information is reprinted with kind permission from Argus Global. Please visit www.argus-global.co.uk for further information.

© Argus Global 2013

Somebody's watching you

Facial scanners, talking vending machines and virtual stores in metro stations... the retail sector's innovation looks revolutionary. But how will consumers react and are there limits to shopper surveillance?

By Virginia Matthews

Biometric face scanners that recognise you from your Facebook page as you enter a store, 'intelligent' kiosks that ask to read your shopping list and suggest recipes for that evening's supper and CCTV systems calibrated to alert sales staff if you loiter too long at a fixture. It sounds like something out of Steven Spielberg's *Minority Report* – in which Tom Cruise has a retinal scan at a shopping mall before he is greeted personally by a video advert recommending he tries a Guinness – but science fiction is already fact in the 21st-century British High Street. Some of the reconnaissance techniques already available, or currently on trial, at a store near you will doubtless raise the hackles of privacy campaigners. Yet the hi-tech gizmos being deployed include other innovations that may be celebrated rather than slated – 3D augmented reality software to help you try before you buy (Tesco and Harrods), so-called magic mirrors instead of changing rooms (Marks & Spencer, John Lewis and New Look), Quick Response barcodes tracing the provenance of a particular garment back to the weaver (IOU Project) or in-store sat-nav to help you find your way around (Tesco).

As stores wrestle with the challenging complexities of simultaneous bricks-and-mortar, web and mobile retailing – or what David Martin, joint managing director of brand design agency M Worldwide, calls an 'immersive, multichannel consumer experience' – the bumper opportunities for the electronics sector are clear. But are some of the more invasive techniques of the security industry appropriate for the High Street? Global IT consultancy Wipro is exploring the privacy implications of a new in-store digital kiosk which identifies shoppers via photographs they post on Facebook and other social networks, and then uses that information to target them when they enter a store. It firmly believes such moves are entirely logical. 'We're all used to having cameras in stores and we've become accustomed to being recorded,' says Vivek Venugopalan, chief technologist for retail and consumer packaged goods at the Bangalore-based tech firm, 'but the question now is whether it makes sense for retailers to throw away all that valuable footage or apply it to improving the retail environment. I'm not suggesting that entries on Facebook would be used commercially without a person's knowledge – opt-in will be essential – but our experience is that younger people, in particular, are willing to trade personal information for better, more targeted offers. We're merely joining the dots between online and offline shopping experiences.'

Digital generation

Venugopalan believes that the inexorable rise of the smartphone – now used by one in three adults in the UK according to telecoms regulator Ofcom – is the perfect conduit for dovetailing the needs of retailers and customers. 'Younger people love their phones and are more au fait with digital technology,' he says. 'They are the key target for a host of new mobile solutions that will soon allow them to order and pay for products virtually and instantly as they pass a shop window or poster hoarding, simply by pointing their phone at them.' While Wipro is now 'aggressively targeting UK retailers' with its recognition system – and believes the first trial will begin here within 18 months – it was a children's charity that made UK history in February with the first interactive advert. Launched by Plan UK, the 40-second ad used facial-scanning technology to distinguish men from women and to offer different messages. Women were targeted with information about female education in poor countries, while men were directed to the charity's website.

Although campaigners from the Open Rights Group called the ad 'creepy', the era of so-called intelligent promotions is long overdue, argues Chris O'Malley, director of retail marketing at Intel Corp. 'While I believe that more sophisticated scanning is the key to retailing's future, the extent to which the new generation of face-recognition technology becomes truly effective depends on the public,' he says. 'Most of the applications of scanning in use in the UK today are anonymised, merely giving information on gender and likely age group. With co-operation from consumers though – who we believe will agree to swipe their phone as they enter a store, as long as there is inducement in the way of additional service or attractive discounts – the applications could become extensive.'

Business intelligence

One of Intel's trailblazers is an interactive vending machine. Developed in the US in association with food giant Kraft, it allows stores to talk directly to shoppers – who must first agree to take part – dispensing free samples of trial lines, offering recipe ideas using Kraft products and driving traffic back to the company's website for further offers. Intel, which is in advanced talks with Sainsbury's, M&S and Tesco regarding a UK trial later this year, believes that the vast majority of the 500,000-plus vending devices in use in Britain can be recalibrated to carry smart software for less than £1,000 each.

There is a sound practical reason why retailers are so keen to progress from general observation of shopping habits to the particular, as Venugopalan points out: 'The truth is that while automatic gender scanning is fairly reliable, age scanning is far more iffy. If you end up insulting someone who looks older than they actually are by suggesting they buy a particular fashion or cosmetics range, they will hardly warm to you.' As arguably the most watched nation in the world, we have long been accustomed to the blink of a CCTV system recording our every move in car parks, streets and stores, but the new application for video surveillance technology is business intelligence, says Jon Cropley, principal analyst at market research firm IMS.

'Video content may be set up to identify individuals spending too long in a particularly vulnerable area such as the back of the store and that information can be invaluable if you are losing millions of pounds each year to shrinkage,' he says. While theft by customers and staff remains a thorny issue for all retail businesses, in-store CCTV can also be used to understand shopper behaviour or, in the case of a number of Las Vegas casinos, quickly identify known high-rollers and remind staff to extend a warm welcome to them. Cropley believes that the use of CCTV may even 'improve the overall customer experience for all of us'. Using what he calls a 'loitering algorithm', a monitoring system can alert staff if a customer is seen spending a disproportionate amount of time at a particular fixture – electronics, say – and can immediately send in expert staff to 'help and advise'. Other applications would include identifying the busiest parts of the store, using the resulting data to sell strategic store positions to third parties for higher rates. Stock level and in-house promotion planning would also benefit from such tracking, Cropley believes. 'We are already seeing a lot of interest among High Street food,

clothing and electronics retailers who believe that the long-term returns of this kind of shopper surveillance are very attractive,' he adds.

Clicks to bricks

Martin at M Worldwide understands the dynamics of retail layout and the intricacies of so-called power aisles (the prime locations in a store), decompression zones (areas just inside the entrance) and the ways in which companies can capitalise on the fact that 75 per cent of us automatically look right when entering a store. He believes that while more of the transactional cut-and-thrust of shopping will inevitably happen online in the future, traditional stores still have an important part to play in terms of 'retail theatre'.

'As the more mundane aspects of shopping are done virtually, often via your phone, aimless aisle-walking past rows and rows of white goods or sofas will become a thing of the past,' Martin adds, suggesting that the space currently given over to larger items will be used to stage cookery, DIY or grow-your-own gardening events that showcase products in the store. 'Despite High Street occupancy being at an all-time low and Internet shopping growing exponentially, traditional bricks and mortar remain the lifeblood of the retail sector,' he explains. 'And even the most committed online retailers are turning to traditional environments so they can offer a more rounded experience.' Proof of Martin's clicks-to-bricks argument comes with the announcement by Amazon of its first physical store, in Seattle in the US – selling tablets and readers and, ironically, offering a 'hands-on experience of its products'. But there are other intriguing approaches, too. Last summer, Tesco Homeplus converted Seoul's Hangangjin metro station into the world's first fully functioning virtual store, boosting its online sales in the country by 130 per cent. The trial, which involved transforming the walls of the station into virtual displays of products, each with its own scannable (by phone) QR barcode, and which established

same-day home delivery as the norm, is now being rolled out at 20 bus stops in the city

Tesco's international spokesman Ian Hutchins believes a similar move in Britain is possible. 'Although no announcement around a UK virtual store experiment is imminent, the extension of our trial in [South] Korea is a clear indication that we see this as a potentially successful business model. In terms of a UK rollout, I certainly wouldn't rule anything out,' he says. If Martin is correct, those of us with smartphones – and the will to use them co-operatively with the retail brands that rank highly in our lives – are already in sight of a retailing revolution. But even he isn't convinced that the dazzling array of breakthrough technology – including price tags in Brazil that play appropriate music when you try on clothes – is always as significant as some reckon. 'I see a lot of gimmickry by companies that have never innovated, never really developed their offer and will continue to trail behind the blue-chip firms whatever technology they employ,' he says.

As the patchily applied convergence between online and offline shopping by key names on the High Street continues to both amaze and infuriate us, one thing seems certain. However firmly a store aligns itself to the latest IT wizardry, no amount of smoke and (magic) mirrors will turn a mediocre retail brand into a great one. And if you really don't want to be scanned, tracked, monitored and addressed by name as you put away your car keys and reach for a trolley, turn off your phone before you enter a store.

May 2012

⇨ The above information is reprinted with kind permission from *Director magazine*. Please visit www.director.co.uk for further information.

More than 200 schools use CCTV cameras in toilets or changing rooms, claim Big Brother Watch

More than 200 schools are using CCTV cameras in toilets or changing rooms.

A total of 825 cameras were located in the toilets or changing rooms of 207 schools across England, Scotland and Wales, figures provided by more than 2,000 schools showed.

Almost one in ten of the schools which use CCTV said cameras were positioned in such places, while 54 have more than one camera for every 15 students.

Nick Pickles, director of Big Brother Watch, said: 'This research raises serious questions about the privacy of schoolchildren across Britain, with some schools having one camera for every five pupils

and hundreds of schools using cameras in toilets and changing rooms.

'The full extent of school surveillance is far higher than we had expected and will come as a shock to many parents.

'Schools need to come clean about why they are using these cameras and what is happening to the footage.

'Local authorities also need to be doing far more to reign in excessive surveillance in their areas and ensuring resources are not being diverted from more effective alternatives.'

Hardial Hayer, headteacher at The Radclyffe School, which has 20 cameras, said the CCTV was in place for safeguarding children.

'The cameras do not have any impact on anybody's privacy,' he told *The Huffington Post UK*. 'They just see students entering the toilets. We are open about having the cameras – we tell all the parents and the students have said they feel safer.

'Very often children congregate in the toilets and make other pupils feel intimidated. With the cameras we always know how many are in there.

Big Brother Watch, which published the figures following a Freedom of

Information Act request, also warned that the Home Office's proposals for a new regulatory structure was 'not fit for purpose'.

The new post of Surveillance Camera Commissioner 'will have absolutely no powers to do anything', Pickles added.

'Parents will be right to say that such a woefully weak system is not good enough.'

Responses from 2,107 secondary schools and academies showed they used 47,806 cameras, including 26,887 inside school buildings.

With 1.8 million pupils being taught in these schools, there was an average of one camera for every 38 children.

In all, 90% of schools had CCTV cameras, with an average of 24 cameras in each of the 1,537 secondary schools that responded and 30 cameras in each of the 570 academies.

The estimated number of CCTV cameras in secondary schools and academies across England, Wales and Scotland was now 106,710, the campaigners said.

The table below demonstrates the ten schools with the most cameras. Headteacher Hayer added the reason the school is at the top of the list is due to having 20 small toilet blocks, rather than a few large ones.

'The cameras mean the school is a safe environment. It has been a huge success.'

A spokesperson for the National Association of Head Teachers (NAHT), said schools that use CCTV must ensure the cameras 'are placed sensitively'.

'It is important that parents and pupils are fully aware that cameras are present and that issues of who monitors, and what happens to, the resulting footage are clear in the home–school agreement,' the spokesperson said.

'It is always a balance between preserving an individual's right to privacy with their right not to be maliciously targeted in inaccessible areas of the school.

'Most schools will be aware of these conflicts and aim to manage each situation on its merits.'

A Department for Education spokesperson said: 'Schools using CCTV are required by law to adhere to the Data Protection Act. 'We have already acted to make it unlawful for schools to use biometric data like fingerprints without parents' permission. CCTV can be beneficial in some cases but this is a decision that head teachers should take.'

The school with the least students per camera was Christ The King Catholic and Church of England (VA) Centre for Learning, Knowsley, in the north-west of England, which had five students per camera.

The school could not be reached for comment.

12 September 2012

⇨ The above information is reprinted with kind permission from *The Huffington Post*. Please visit www.huffingtonpost.co.uk for further information.

Ten schools in the UK with the most CCTV cameras

	School	Location	CCTV Cameras
1	The Radclyffe School	Oldham, North West	20
2	St Mary's Church of England High School (VA)	Hertfordshire, East of England	18
3	The Fairy School	Staffordshire, West Midlands	14
4	Wildern School	Hampshire, South East	12
5	Ecclesfield School	Sheffield, Yorkshire & Humberside	12
6	Portland School	Nottinghamshire, East Midlands	12
7	King Ecgbert School	Sheffield, Yorkshire & Humberside	12
8	Montgomery High School	Blackpool, North West	12
9	St Wilfred's Catholic High School & 6th Form	Wakefield, Yorkshire & Humberside	12
10	Thomas Deacon Academy	Peterborough, East Midlands	12

In the middle of our street

By Natalie Hart and Hannah Thompson

Many of our respondents see Google Street View as an extremely useful tool, but some feel uneasy about its alleged breaches of privacy, objecting to the actual photographing of streets as well as to allegations of Google's collection of other private data, responses to our question on the issue have shown.

Many respondents were specific about how they use the interactive map

'I use it to work out tricky routes'

'I like to see where my family abroad lives'

'I use it to check out B&Bs before going on holiday'

'I use it to look at properties to buy or rent'

'Helpful'

'It's an excellent concept and very useful'

However, some respondents were concerned about just how private Google's data gathering is, amid revelations earlier this year that 'Google cars' touring countries for images unintentionally gathered data including passwords, snippets of emails, email addresses, text or even the website page that the WiFi user may have been viewing at that moment, through unsecured WiFi networks.

'I was alarmed at the data they have gathered'

'There is no excuse for this'

'I don't like the lack of privacy'

'You can clearly see my ten-year-old son in the window [in the image of my house]'

'Teething problem'

'Google should be tried for espionage'

Meanwhile, others excuse such data collection error as 'a little glitch' and 'teething problem' with the service, while some pointed out that information on 'unsecured networks is already in the public domain' and claim that the problem is with 'the WiFi company not Google'.

Privacy problems

The debate comes within the global context of Google's reputation as a firm which could do more to protect users' privacy. Soon after it launched in 2007, it came near the bottom of a Privacy International report on large companies' records on privacy; earlier this year Australian police launched an investigation following reports of private data gathering and the company has received worldwide criticism, including from governments and residents of Germany, Japan, Canada and the UK.

Google has maintained that any private data were collected in error and have been destroyed, but this month saw the UK's Information Commissioner ruling that the company was in 'significant breach' of the Data Protection Act and will face an audit into its practices.

10 November 2011

⇨ The above information is reprinted with kind permission from YouGov. Please visit www.yougov.co.uk for further information.

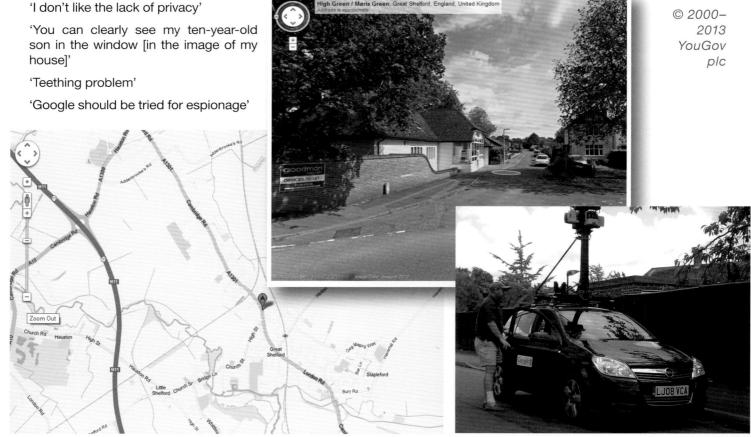

© 2000–2013 YouGov plc

Google Street View 'shows homes despite privacy requests'

Google has been accused of 'sheer arrogance' by security-conscious residents of Carshalton in Surrey after it apparently ignored requests for privacy and published photographs of their homes from its Street View service.

By Christopher Williams

More than half a dozen homeowners in Warnham Court Road asked the web giant not to post images of their properties online after it introduced Street View to Britain in 2009 over fears they could be used by burglars. Google duly removed the photographs.

When Tim Jury, a company director, recently checked on the website, however, he found the Street View car had revisited Warnham Court Road and updated the web with unfettered views of his and neighbours' homes.

'I think it's plain wrong,' he said. 'We had a leaflet from the police a few days ago saying there had been 13 burglaries in the area and people are worried about security.'

'Google is a technology company; it ought to be easy for them to ensure they keep blurring properties when they update the images.'

Mr Jury was forced to reapply for the image of his house, and that of an elderly neighbour who does not have Internet access, to be blurred. He repeatedly asked Google why it had published them despite his earlier request but received no reply.

'It's the sheer arrogance of not responding,' he said. 'I can't believe an organisation like that can't answer some simple questions.'

Mr Jury even visited Google's London offices but was told by a security guard to make his complaints to the police.

This week Google announced its fleet of Street View cars, which are fitted with 360-degree rooftop cameras, had been roaming Britain again and it had updated its images.

The Information Commissioner's Office, Britain's privacy watchdog, which has investigated Street View before for intercepting passwords and other sensitive data from WiFi networks, said Google should not have published the new photographs.

'While the picture of a building would not be classed as personal data – and therefore would not normally be covered by the Data Protection Act – it is reasonable to expect Google to have measures in place so that people who have asked for their house to be removed from Google Street View, do not have to send in repeated requests every time the images are updated,' a spokesman said.

'If Google are failing to provide this service then they should not be surprised when people express their concern.'

Google said it would investigate Mr Jury's complaints.

Images which have been blurred following a user's request should remain blurred when imagery of an area is refreshed,' a spokesman said.

'If users notice anything unusual, for example their house reappears after it has been blurred, we encourage them to notify us using the same reporting tool so that we can investigate it promptly.'

8 March 2013

⇨ The above information is reprinted with kind permission from *The Daily Telegraph*. Please visit www.telegraph. co.uk for further information.

Key facts

- Article 8 of the UK's Human Rights Act is a broad-ranging right that is often closely connected with other rights such as freedom of religion, freedom of expression, freedom of association and the right to respect for property. (page 1)

- The notion of privacy first emerged in Britain during the 16th century as a result of changes in the design of the home. Before then, the majority of homes had consisted of a single shared space where family and household members slept, cooked, ate and worked together. (page 2)

- Privacy as we know it is a relatively modern concept that was 'invented' around 400 years ago. Every time privacy has developed another layer of meaning, it has been in response to the introduction of a new technology into people's lives – from the chimney, to the camera and printing press, to the Internet. (page 2)

- There are now more than 80 million mobile phone subscriptions in the UK. Over a quarter of UK adults are smartphone users, with 60 per cent buying their phone in the last year. Data volumes transferred over mobile networks increased by 67 per cent in 2010. (page 5)

- In recent years the Government has lost 25 million child benefit records as well as the personal information of those serving in the armed forces, witnesses in criminal cases and prisoners. (page 7)

- 50% of the public believe that the Government's draft Communications Data Bill is poor value for money. (page 8)

- Although over four in ten (41%) people said they would be less likely to use online services and websites if they knew their activity was being recorded, almost half (48%) of Britons said this would make no difference. (page 8)

- Only 13% of respondents indicated that they fully understood how cookies work, 37% had heard of Internet cookies but did not understand how they work and 2% of people had not heard of Internet cookies before participating in the survey. (page 9)

- The Data Protection Act gives you the right to find out what information the Government and other organisations stores about you. (page 11)

- Key facts from Google's Transparency Report, June – December 2012: the UK made 1,458 requests – 70% of which resulted in some form of data being produced. Canada, Switzerland and Denmark made the least number of requests. The highest percentages of requests that resulted in some form of data being released, were from Singapore, Taiwan, the UK and the United States. Only 1% of requests in Russia were granted data release. (page 13)

- Between 1 April 2012 and 30 September 2012 the National DNA Database produced 61 matches to murder, 225 to rapes and 12,537 to other crime scenes. (page 14)

- 59% of consumers were aware that companies can gather information from personal profiles on social networking websites (rising to 68% of Internet users with a social networking profile). (page 17)

- 66% of Internet users felt more should be done to protect their personal information on the Internet. (page 18)

- It is estimated that over £38 billion is lost within the UK to fraud, with £0.54 billion lost to online ticketing scams and bogus career opportunity offers – types of fraud young people aged 18–25 suffer from the most. (page 21)

- Respondents were asked whether they had ever read a privacy policy. In total 40% of respondents had, meaning 60% of young people have not read the privacy policies of the web sites they use … When those who had not read a policy were asked why not, there were a variety of responses: 32% said they didn't know what a privacy policy was, with 23% saying they didn't know where to find it. A quarter felt they were too complicated, and another quarter did not feel it important. (page 25)

- One in three people (37%) said their support for CCTV had increased following the London riots in 2011. (page 29)

- A total of 825 cameras were located in the toilets or changing rooms of 207 schools across England, Scotland and Wales, figures provided by more than 2,000 schools showed. (page 36)

Big Brother

The term comes from a character in George Orwell's novel *Nineteen Eighty-Four*, from which the phrase 'Big Brother is watching you' originated. Big Brother embodied totalitarianism; a regime where the government controls and monitors every aspect of people's lives and behaviour.

Biometric data

Biometrics (or biometric authentication) refers to a method of uniquely identifying people. This includes methods such as fingerprints, DNA, retinal scans (eyes) and facial recognition; something that is permanent throughout a person's lifetime and doesn't change as they age. The main uses of biometric data are for the purpose of controlling access (e.g. some laptops have fingerprint scanners) or helping tackle and prevent crime.

CCTV

Closed-circuit television (CCTV) is the use of mounted video cameras which broadcast a live image to a television screen closely watched over by someone (can be recorded). CCTV is used to observe an area in an effort to reduce and prevent crime. However, the use of CCTV has triggered a debate about security versus privacy.

Communication Data Bill

This legislation would mean that Internet service provider (ISP) and mobile phone services would be able to gather much more data about what their customers are doing. Currently, communication monitoring is limited to data such as who people send emails to and who they ring, not the actual content of the messages themselves, for 12 months. This Bill would extend it to webmail, voice calls, social media and Internet gaming. This is why it has been labelled as the 'Snooper's Charter'. It is estimated to cost approximately £1.8 billion.

Data Protection Act 1988 (DPA)

This act exists to protect personal information about people. It ensures that personal data is kept secure, accurate and up-to-date. You can ask to see data about you (the 'right of access'), but not other peoples. Other people cannot ask to see data about you. The organisation has up to 40 days to reply to your request. You have the right to know why that data is being held, where the data has come from and if any automated decisions are being made about you using this data.

DNA

Deoxyribonucleic acid (DNA) contains genetic information that is unique to each individual. This means it is possible to identify someone from a sample of their DNA, such as a hair or skin sample. By having this information, a DNA record can be matched to a DNA sample found at a crime scene and therefore makes it easier to find the criminal.

DNA database/United Kingdom National DNA Database

The UK has a national database of DNA profiles which the police can use to match suspect DNA. Samples are taken from crime scenes, police suspects and anyone arrested and detained at a police station (in England and Wales). The database has helped in solving both past and present crimes. However, controversial privacy issues about the DNA database have arisen because samples have been taken and held onto from people who are innocent and some people feel that they should be removed/destroyed from the database. In March 2012 the database is estimated to contain almost six million individual records.

Article 8: Right to privacy

Article 8 of the European Convention on Human Rights states that 'Everyone has the right for his private and family life, his home and his correspondence.' There are some exceptions to this rule however, so this means that your right to privacy can be interfered with as long as it is 'in accordance with law' and 'necessary in a democratic society'.

Regulation of Investigatory Powers Act 2000 (RIPA)

RIPA is the law governing the use of covert techniques, such as surveillance and investigation, by public authorities. This means that when public authorities, such as the police or government departments, need to use covert techniques to obtain private information, they do it in a way that is respectful of human rights and only when really necessary. For example, it could be used in the case of a terror alert, for the purposes of detecting crime or even for public safety.

Surveillance

The close observation and monitoring of behaviour or activities. To keep watch over a person or group. The UK has been described as a 'surveillance society' because of its large number of CCTV cameras and the national DNA database; the UK was once referred to as 'the most surveilled country' in the Western states.

Protection of Freedoms Act 2012

An act that regulates the use of biometric data, the use of surveillance and many other things. For example, this will mean schools need to get parents' consent before processing child's biometric information and it also introduces a code of practice for surveillance camera systems. Essentially, this is to help protect people from state intrusion in their lives.

Assignments

1. Design a poster to demonstrate the eight rules of the Data Protection Act.

2. Look up the Human Convention, article 8 *Right to Privacy*. Find out what the Universal Declaration of Human Rights (1948) says about the right to privacy. Can you think of any situations in your own experience where this right has not been observed? You might find *Right to a private and family life* on page 1 useful. Discuss in pairs.

3. Using a map, create an illustrated diagram comparing and contrasting different worldviews on privacy – what might be law in Great Britain, might be completely different in somewhere like China. See *The invention of privacy* on page 2 for further information.

4. 'Big Brother is watching you.' What does the phrase 'Big Brother' mean? Discuss in groups.

5. Research surveillance drones: are they an invasion of privacy or a useful tool for law enforcement and research? Debate this in pairs and feedback to the rest of your class.

6. Choose a partner. Using the Internet, research your partner from the perspective of someone who doesn't already know them and note down what you find out about them. You could try typing their name into a search engine and having a look at social media sites such as Facebook or Twitter. How much information have you found? Do you think your partner takes enough care with their online safety? Give them some feedback.

7. Do you think the Communication Data Bill should become law, or not? Decide whether you are in favour of the bill or against it and produce a leaflet that demonstrates your perspective. In the leaflet, you should explain what the Communications Data Bill is and what would it do. You should also explain the reasons behind your view point. The aim of the leaflet is to persuade others that your opinion is right. Bear this in mind when you are writing. You might find the articles on pages 6, 7 and 8 useful.

8. Write an article for your school or college magazine entitled *What are biometrics and how do they work?*. Use the information on page 33, as well as your own research.

9. Write a short story about what the future would be like if a government who abused technology such as CCTV, ID cards and the DNA database came to power. How might they use these things to control citizens? What would life be like for people living in this future society? Your story should be at least 700 words.

10. Make a list of all the organisations you think hold personal data about you. Choose one of those organisations and look at the terms and conditions that you agree to when you sign up. Read the terms and conditions carefully. Have you accidentally agreed to share your information with a third party? What other conditions have you agreed to? Is there anything that surprises you? What implications might this have in the future? Make some notes and feed back to the rest of your class.

11. Imagine that your local MP has begun a campaign to double the amount of CCTV cameras in your town. Do you think CCTV cameras are a useful crime fighting tool or an invasion of personal privacy? Write a letter to your MP either supporting their campaign, or explaining why you disagree with it.

12. Debate the following motion in two groups, with one arguing in favour and the other against: 'This house believes that increased surveillance measures such as CCTV are a small price to pay to prevent terrorist attacks.'

13. Many young people are unaware of the risks involved when submitting personal information to websites. Design a series of banner or rollover ads which could be displayed on a site where young people might submit personal information, for example a social networking site. These ads should highlight the dangers of carelessly uploading personal information and provide some worst-case scenarios.

14. Choose a celebrity and follow their magazine and newspaper coverage over the course of a month. Cut/print out relevant photos and extracts and make a scrap book. Review the coverage they have received. Is it mostly positive or negative? Do you think it invades the celebrity's privacy in any way? Or do you think they invite invasion of their private life by behaving a certain way?

15. Your school has announced that they will install CCTV cameras around the building, including in toilets and changing rooms, in an effort to help prevent bullying and make students feel safer. Are you for or against this motion? Do the benefits of safety outweigh the potential invasion of privacy?

Acknowledgements

The publisher is grateful for permission to reproduce the following material.

While every care has been taken to trace and acknowledge copyright, the publisher tenders its apology for any accidental infringement or where copyright has proved untraceable. The publisher would be pleased to come to a suitable arrangement in any such case with the rightful owner.

Chapter 1: Privacy and the law

Right to a private and family life © Liberty 2013, *The invention of privacy* © The Futures Company 2013, *Data protection and privacy laws* © Privacy International, *Communications Data Bill published* © Crown Copyright 2013, *Twitter, Virgin Media, O2 and ISPA slam data-snooping bill* © ComputerworldUK 2013, *Snoopers' Charter mythbuster* © Liberty 2013, *Communications Data Bill survey* © 2000 – 2013 YouGov plc, *Guidance on the rules and use of cookies and similar technologies* © Information Commissioner's Office 2012.

Chapter 2: Personal data

The Data Protection Act © Crown Copyright 2013, *The big debate: open data* © 2013 Guardian News and Media Limited, *Key facts from Google's Transparency Report, June – December 2012* © Cara Acred/Independence Educational Publishers Ltd., *The National DNA Database* © Crown Copyright 2013, *Eight million UK children on secret database without parental consent* © 2012 digitaljournal.com, *Online personal data: the consumer perspective* © Communications Consumer Panel 2011, *Why you should be concerned about privacy online* © 2013 Knowthenet.org.uk, *Careless generation* © Action Fraud 2013, *Facebook's Generation Y nightmare* © 2013 Guardian News and Media Limited, *Facebook and you* © 2000 – 2013 YouGov plc., *Children and online privacy survey* © the i in online 2011, *Should parents spy on their children's emails and texts?* © Judith Woods/The Daily Telegraph 2013.

Chapter 3: Surveillance

CCTV images: exploding the myths © CCTV User Group 2011, *Crowdsourcing crime prevention* © InternetEyes Limited 2012, *CCTV and Big Brother* ©

2013 AOL (UK) Limited, *Surveillance camera code of practice consultation* © Crown Copyright 2013, *State surveillance* © Liberty 2013, *What is biometrics?* © Argus Global 2013, *Somebody's watching you* © 2013 Director Publications, *More than 200 schools use CCTV cameras in toilets or changing rooms claim Big Brother Watch* © 2013 AOL (UK) Limited, *In the middle of our street* © 2000 – 2013 YouGov plc, *Google Street View 'shows homes despite privacy requests'* © Christopher Williams/The Daily Telegraph 2013.

Illustrations:

Pages 11 & 19: Don Hatcher; pages 25 & 39: Angelo Madrid; pages 16 & 30: Simon Kneebone.

Images:

Cover and pages i & 29 © Karen Barefoot, page 10 © Jamie Anne, page 12 & 13 © Loops7, page 21 © Erik Elena, page 33 © Lorendana Bejerita, page 36 © Matt, page 38 (left and middle) © Google Street View, page 39 (right) © Bally Hoo.

Additional acknowledgements:

Editorial on behalf of Independence Educational Publishers by Cara Acred.

With thanks to the Independence team: Mary Chapman, Sandra Dennis, Christina Hughes, Jackie Staines and Jan Sunderland.

Cara Acred

Cambridge

May 2013